CASES IN COMPUTER INFORMATION SYSTEMS

The manuscript for this book was prepared on an IBM® PC and submitted in electronic form. It was designed and set at Holt, Rinehart and Winston, Inc. on a Macintosh™ Plus computer using Microsoft Word™. Output was generated on an Apple® LaserWriter™ Plus.

CASES IN COMPUTER INFORMATION SYSTEMS

BARRY SHORE
University of New Hampshire

JERRY RALYA

HOLT, RINEHART AND WINSTON, INC.

New York Chicago San Francisco Philadelphia
Montreal Toronto London Sydney Tokyo

ISBN 0-03-007744-3

Printed in the United States of America

8 9 0 1 090 9 8 7 6 5 4 3 2

Holt, Rinehart and Winston, Inc.
The Dryden Press
Saunders College Publishing

PREFACE

The introductory course in computers and information systems is an ideal time to provide students with the opportunity to apply what they have learned. There are two ways that this can be done. First, cases can be used to illustrate how concepts and skills can be applied to realistic settings; second, students can be given hands-on computer exercises involving word processing, spreadsheets, and data management. This Casebook does both. It is designed to be used as a supplement and complement to existing introductory textbooks.

The purpose of this Casebook is to provide realistic examples as well as practice in the ways that computer information systems are used and developed by today's organizations. Cases are presented that show how computer information systems can help firms operate more efficiently and assist management in making better decisions.

In the first sections of the book, the cases offer an overview of typical computer information system applications and associated problems, and are also intended to help the student better understand how computer hardware and software function. More specific areas of interest follow, in sections on such topics as data input and output, the use of database management systems, topics in office automation, the use of electronic spreadsheets, and artificial intelligence. The book's organization makes it straightforward to identify appropriate cases for a topic covered in a syllabus. Cases can be used in any order.

In all, 41 cases are presented, spread across the complete spectrum of contemporary information system use. Throughout, an end-user's point of view is adopted, along with the assumption that the successful business professional must be an active rather than a passive user of computer information systems. Special attention is paid to the integral role of microcomputers in today's organizations.

The cases are fictionalized accounts of typical real-life situations. They were developed in this way so that they could focus on teaching goals. The cases are not lengthy, and when used in class will require from 10 minutes to half an hour, depending on the instructor's objectives in using the case.

Another reason that the cases have been developed as fictionalized accounts is that reports of real cases often have too much technical detail for the beginning student to grasp. The cases in this book are written so that the student will have no trouble understanding the technical environment once the material in an introductory text has been read. In fact, most cases include definitions when a new technical term is introduced, and also develop conveptual frameworks within the case; the glossary at the end of the book also defines technical terms. In other words, the Casebook is very close to self-sufficient.

Cases can be used in a variety of ways. Since they are all but self-sufficient, they can serve as a review for the student while illustrating how to apply the skills and concepts covered in a textbook. One way to use the cases, then, is to assign them after the corresponding chapter of the introductory text has been covered.

Cases can equally well be used to motivate a chapter in the textbook. The chapter material and case can be assigned together, and the case discussed before the chapter is covered in detail. According to one model of learning behavior, this approach motivates the student to learn more about a topic, and as a result the student may be more receptive to the material covered in the following class discussion.

Whichever way the cases are used, students should be required to write answers for each of the questions and bring the written answers to class. The better prepared the students are, the better will be the case discussion, and the richer will be the educational experience.

The cases and technical material cover up-to-date issues and technical topics. From the new IBM PS/2 microcomputer line to networks, artificial intelligence, and computer graphics, students have the opportunity to become involved in timely, user-related issues. We hope that you enjoy and benefit from using these cases.

Barry Shore
Portsmouth, New Hampshire

Jerry Ralya
New York City

CONTENTS

SECTION 1

INTRODUCTION
AND
OVERVIEW

Computer information systems are found today in virtually every organization. Manufacturers, service firms, government agencies, and nonprofit organizations all rely upon computer information systems to collect, store, process, and present information to support their information needs.

In this first section of the Casebook, some representative examples are given of how computer information systems are used. The first case, Central Electronics, describes a medium-sized business on the verge of automating its inventory. At North American Food Company, the large corporation of the second case, automation is already routine, but not for a user who wants up-to-date reports for tracking sales and market share data; the route taken in this case -- doing it oneself -- is becoming increasingly common today. The final case in the Introduction and Overview section, West Side Accountants, shows a small firm taking its first tentative steps into the microcomputer age.

CENTRAL ELECTRONICS

Central Records, located in a major midwestern city, was founded by Bill Terrance and Mary Alice McKay over five years ago. Mary Alice brought most of the business skills to the partnership, while Bill brought a flair for upscale merchandising. The store, which had over 10,000 square feet of selling space, included a wide selection of records, from rock and pop to classical and jazz. The prices were all discounted, and the decor was dramatic. Flashing neon lights, a large-screen video system located in each of the seven different record departments, and a $100,000 sound system created more than just an atmosphere in which customers could buy records. The store itself was entertainment!

Central Records became very successful. Annual sales grew to over $5 million. But last year Mary Alice grew restlesss and was anxious to try something new. Bill agreed.

NEW BUSINESS: DISCOUNT ELECTRONICS

Six months ago Mary Alice and Bill opened Central Electronics, a discount electronics warehouse. Central Electronics sold music systems, TVs, computers, telephone answering machines, and small computers. Again, using his flair for merchandising, Bill created an atmosphere that was different from that found in most other stores, especially the large chains. And because of this interesting atmosphere and discount prices, business flourished.

But the electronics business was quite different from the record business. One major distinction was that the cost of most items, such as compact disk players and computers, was much higher than the cost of a record. As a result the investment in inventory in the electronics store was more than five times as great as in the record store.

Mary Alice was aware that the profitability of the electronics store depended heavily on the ability to have good information about the stock. Central Electronics needed to know what items were in stock and what items were on order.

At the present time the store didn't have the data. If a customer asked for a particular item, and the item was not on the sales floor, then the salesperson had to call the inventory clerks in the back of the warehouse. Sometimes it could take ten minutes to find out if an item was in stock, and occasionally the clerk would even return the wrong information. In addition to the fact that inventory data were not accessible to the sales staff, there was also little inventory data that the order department could use to monitor inventory levels and place reorders. It troubled Mary Alice that her staff had little control over this critical resource. Just a week before she had asked Bill how a store that sells computers could justify not using them. And with sales for the last month exceeding her forecast by 37 percent, Mary Alice was convinced that the time to act had come.

A COMPUTER FOR CENTRAL

Ann Breyer, a sales representative for a computer manufacturer, was beginning her sales presentation. A week ago Mary Alice had called and briefed Ann on the problems at Central Electronics.

"Mary Alice, let me show you what I came up with," Ann began. "After talking with some of the sales reps in the office, here is the system we propose. To begin, the system will support point-of-sale terminals at the sales counters and terminals in the warehouse area and offices.

"The point-of-sale terminals will be located at your checkout stations on the sales floor. When an item is purchased an optical wand will be passed over the bar code label that will be affixed to every inventory item. This wand will read the bar code and the point-of-sale terminal will then display the product description and price on its screen.

"Not only will this speed customer checkout and reduce errors, but the data will be used to update inventory records. You will then have better records of the items you sell and will be able to produce regular reports, which can be used for reordering or controlling your investment in inventory."

Bill had been quietly listening in. "Ann, I don't know much about computers, but I do need to know what it is we will be buying and what it is this equipment will do for us," he said.

"Our recommendation is a minicomputer that will give you the computer power to meet your present and future needs," Ann replied. She showed Bill and Mary Alice a digram (Figure 1). It represents the smallest of our minicomputers, and will be able to support as many as twelve terminals, which can be connected to the mini through cables. At the beginning I think you will need ten terminals -- two in the offices, three in the warehouse, and five on the retail floor. In addition to the mini and the ten terminals, I am also recommending a hard disk, which will be used to store all the software that will be needed as well as the bar code reference data and inventory database. And I have also included a printer that will be used to obtain written reports -- we call this **hard copy**. Bill, the collection of all this equipment is called the **hardware**."

"Is that all there is to it?" Bill asked.

"No," Ann said. "In addition to describing the system in hardware terms, let's look at it from a functional point of view. Let's divide your data processing activities into input, output, processing, and storage. We call this the **data**

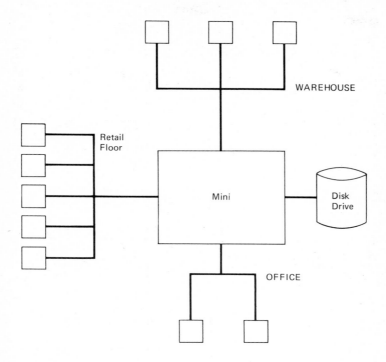

WAREHOUSE

Retail
Floor

Mini

Disk
Drive

OFFICE

Figure 1. The computer system at Central Electronics will include termimals in the retail area, warehouse, and offices.

processing cycle. The cycle begins when someone wants to enter data into the system. This input might be entered through the optical wand as it is reading bar code or it might be entered into a terminal when a shipment of new equipment arrives from one of your suppliers. In inventory, an input would be required if a stockroom clerk needs to find out if a telephone answering machine is in stock. In this situation the inventory number would be typed on the keyboard of the terminal. Or if a stereo receiver is taken from the stockroom shelf, then the clerk would also enter the corresponding data as input into the keyboard. So every time data are needed, or whenever data must be entered, an appropriate entry will be made through one of these ten terminals."

"I think I follow you so far," Bill said. "I'm trying, anyway."

"Good!" Ann said. "Let's pause for a moment on what happens once the data are entered. The **central processing unit** -- the **CPU** -- of the computer is responsible for processing requests made through the terminals. So if a sales clerk is about to make a sale, the optical wand is moved over the bar code label; the data are then sent to the CPU; there software instructs the system to look up the bar code, in a table where the price associated with that code is found. The software then instructs the system to return the price to the screen of the point-of-sale terminal. The CPU also processes the data to update the inventory record in the database. Once this update is made the inventory database will then reflect the up-to-the-minute level of inventory.

"As you can see, the CPU receives its instructions from **software**, or programs that provide instructions for the operation of the computer," Ann went on. "There are actually two sets of software. One set, called **system software**, is used to manage the internal activities of the CPU, the terminals, printers, and storage devices. The second set of software, called **application software**, includes specific instructions to perform a business task."

"Who supplies this software?" Bill asked.

"We do," Ann said. "We supply both the system software and the application software. The application software, in this case, will include all the computer instructions necessary to accommodate the kinds of inventory transactions that you will need to undertake, and to produce the kinds of reports you will need to receive.

"The point-of-sale terminals, the conventional terminals used in the offices and in the inventory area, and the printer will provide you with the output you will need. In fact, it is this output that is the most important part of the system. We will work with you to give you the kind of data needed so that the output screens and reports will be as useful as they possibly can be."

"What do you mean?" Bill asked.

"For example," Ann said, "we can supply you with application software that will produce reports that list all units on order, or that summarize inventory quantity by stock number, or that summarize dollar investment in inventory. And we can work with you so that the design of these reports will be exactly as you would like."

"How will all that data be stored?" asked Mary Alice.

"The CPU has only a small capacity to store data," Ann replied. "And this storage is used only for jobs in progress. Longer-term storage usually occurs on disk. You've probably seen the flexible or 'floppy' disks that are used on personal computers. But your system needs much more storage than floppy disks can accommodate. Consequently, your system will have a hard disk. Data can be recorded on this disk by a process somewhat like the one used to store music on a cassette tape. The data are stored on the hard disk using a magnetic process, and can be read many times or changed if a particular data item needs to be updated."

MAKING A DECISION

After Ann left, Bill and Mary Alice found they had trouble agreeing on a strategy. Bill was reluctant to go ahead with the computer purchase.

"Mary Alice, it seems to me we've gotten along without the computer until now. We have at least a dozen other ways to spend our money. Why spend it on something that may not have such a big impact? Maybe we could get by with our manual system for another year. Hire a few more inventory clerks, say. And besides, I'm not sure a computer will cure our problems. Some better controls and a routing report sent to us from the stockroom might give us the same information as a computer system would. I'd like to put this purchase on hold for at least another six months."

QUESTIONS

1. What business is Central Electronics in? What problem is described in this case?
2. How can a computer system help solve the problem at Central Electronics?
3. Describe the data processing cycle.
4. How will entries be made into the computer system proposed for Central?
5. What is the function of the CPU?
6. Describe the function of system software.
7. What is application software? Give an example.
8. Identify the output hardware which Central could use.
9. Is the CPU used for long-term storage of data? Explain.
10. Why is Bill hesitant about investing in a new computer inventory system?
11. Do you think it would be preferable to install only a point-of-sale system and wait until experience is gained with this system before an inventory system is added? What would be the advantages and disadvantages of such a strategy?
12. Bill has suggested that Central's inventory control problem could be solved by instituting better management controls. And he suggests that this may not require a computer. Do you think that businesses may sometimes try to use a computer to solve a problem that is in fact a management problem?
13. Do you think it would be a good idea for Bill and Mary Alice to ask Ann if she could take them to visit other locations where a system similar to the one proposed is in operation? Would this be a way in which both of them could learn more about the benefits and disadvantages of such a system?
14. Do you think a business professional needs to know all of the technical details behind a computer system (for example, knowing the speed with which it will access data on the hard disk, or understanding how to read a listing of the computer instructions in the system and application software), or would it be enough to understand the system from a functional perspective -- that is, to understand what the system will do for the user?

NORTH AMERICAN FOOD

CORPORATION

More than six months ago Alice Feliciano asked central data processing if anything could be done to provide her with up-to-date reports for tracking sales and market share data. Since then she has heard nothing, and continues to rely on outdated sales data, sometimes as much as six weeks late, and on whatever information she can obtain from the sales reps in the field.

"If we could get up-to-date data we would have better control over our advertising and promotion strategies. We would know how these programs are performing and the impact they're having on our market share." Alice was talking with Sean Woodhall. Both were employed in the marketing department of North American Food Corporation (NAFCO), a producer of cereals, canned goods, and frozen foods. Last year NAFCO generated $5 billion in sales from a product line that included over 400 different items. Sales growth over the last 10 years had averaged 8 percent, and most of this growth came from new product introductions -- on average, about 30 new products each year.

Before a product is added to the line, it undergoes an extensive testing and market trial period. First the product ideas are tested by a consumer panel, and then the product is tested in several market areas. Only after careful analysis of the test data and approval by top management is a product added to the line.

The marketing group for which Alice and Sean worked was responsible for overseeing new product trials. They designed advertising and promotion strategies for each test market, and monitored both the sales of the new product and the sales of those products that would be considered competitive.

"Alice, don't you think we have given them enough time?" Sean asked. She agreed, and proceeded to pick up the phone and dial central DP.

TRY END-USER COMPUTING

John Devito answered. He explained that central DP was overloaded with jobs, most of which had a higher priority than the one sent by Alice, and that they might not get to her job for at least another six months, if at all. John suggested that she consider using a spreadsheet package and developing her own application. He explained that the data she needed were maintained on their new database management system (DBMS), a system that among other things makes data more

COLUMNS

	A	B	C	D	E
ROWS 1		NEW MICROWAVE POPCORN			
2					
3		Oct 1	Oct 8	Oct 15	Oct 21
4	SEATTLE				
5	ALBANY				
6	HOUSTON				

Figure 1. When a problem can fit into a table format a spreadsheet can be used.

accessible to users. The benefit to her would be that the data she needed could be accessed from her microcomputer and automatically entered into her spreadsheet.

John said that if she wanted to give it a try and develop her own application, he might be able to give her a few hours of help. He explained, "If I can get you started developing your own applications, others in your group will give it a try. And after this first effort, you will be experienced enough to help them. The benefit for us at central DP is that our backlog will stop growing so fast. It might even come down if enough users switch to end-user computing as I'm suggesting."

WILL A SPREADSHEET WORK?

Alice was not a complete newcomer in this area. She had used spreadsheet software before. She knew that a spreadsheet was nothing more than a table with rows and columns. To use the software, then, the application would have to be capable of being described in this format. So after the phone call, she sketched a table to see if her problem would fit. The sketch is shown in Figure 1.

The name of the product being tested is written across the first row of the table. Down the first column, in rows 4, 5, 6, and 7, are the locations in which market tests for that particular product are being run. Across row 3 are the weeks during which the tests are to be run.

After experimenting with several different layouts, it appeared to her that the application would certainly fit into a table format and that a spreadsheet would work just fine.

DESIGNING THE SPREADSHEET

Several other people in marketing were using spreadsheet software, but no one had used it in the way she expected to. Most developed their own applications, but entered the data themselves using the keyboard on their microcomputers. As John had suggested, Alice needed to access the central computer and have daily data on sales and market share automatically entered into the spreadsheet. And here is where she needed his help.

To prepare for working with John, Alice began to design the spreadsheet application on her micro. She placed the spreadsheet software disk into the disk drive of her computer and then with the outline of a table appearing on the screen, she proceeded to enter the titles and other labels such as test locations and weekly periods. Finally, she saved her spreadsheet on a floppy disk so that it would be available when John arrived later in the day.

DOWNLOADING THE DATA

John liked the design that Alice had developed, and they were able to move quickly to the task of establishing the procedures that Alice would follow to access the data. In anticipation of this session John had already done some work too, so they were able to successfuly download the mainframe data on the first attempt.

John then turned the keyboard over to Alice, and she downloaded the data for another product. It worked!

THE FINAL VERSION

Before he left, John made one more suggestion. "Why don't you revise your spreadsheet so that it includes your target as well as actual data? This way you will be able to make the comparison between what you wanted to achieve and what it is that you are actually achieving. And one more thing. You might want to use the graphics in the spreadsheet package to graph the target and actual data. The graph will be even easier to read than the table."

One week later Alice modified her spreadsheet to incorporate the target sales data, and familiarized herself with the procedure for graphing spreadsheet data. Graphing the data was quite simple. She specified the rows and columns to be included in the graph, and the spreadsheet software did the rest. The results are shown in Figure 2.

It has now been several months since Alice designed her spreadsheet application. Other people in her group were impressed with the ability to access

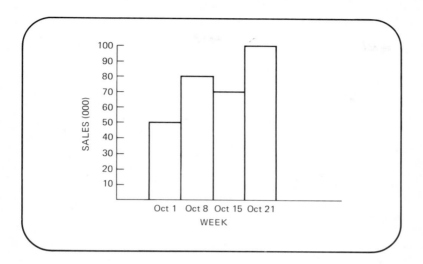

Figure 2. **The output from a spreadsheet can be presented in graphical form.**

mainframe data. Before this project it was impossible for them to get at such data -- in fact, only the central data processing staff with their knowledge of complex computing languages and data-storage details on the mainframe could access the data. Now it seemed that spreadsheets could serve as the interface betwen the professional business staff and the corporate database.

USING THE SPREADSHEET

Alice was very pleased with the performance of her new system. Every day she obtained a new set of graphs depicting the lastest performance of the products for which she was responsible. One week she noticed that one of her products in a particular test market was beginning to fall away from its target. She made some calls and learned that the advertising agency had been lax in placing several newspaper ads. A call to the advertising agency confirmed this, and she worked with them to correct the problem. During the next six weeks, sales for that market recovered and exceeded their target.

Alice was sure that without the immediate feedback from the mainframe data this problem would not have been uncovered and the test results would therefore have been misleading. In fact, the product might have been abandoned. But with the problem corrected in time, and sales exceeding target, management was favorably impressed with the test-market results and the product was introduced six months later. Within a year it became a strong contender in NAFCO's line.

At NAFCO, a new era of end-user computing had begun.

QUESTIONS

1. Define end-user computing.
2. What factors at NAFCO encouraged the use of end-user computing? Do you think other firms suffer similar problems?
3. What are the benefits of end-user computing to the end-user?
4. What are the benefits of end-user computing to central data processing?
5. Describe some of the disadvantages of end-user computing to the end-user.
6. What are the disadvantages of end-user computing to central data processing?
7. Describe the project which Alice undertook.
8. Why was this project more complex than other spreadsheet projects that her colleagues had developed?
9. What factor at the mainframe level made it possible for Alice to successfully develop her application? Do you think that successful end-user computing requires that special system and application software be in place to accommodate the need to access data that are stored beyond a user's microcomputer?
10. Do you think the table would have been all that was needed to present the data, or do you think graphics was needed? When do you think graphics is helpful to the user?
11. The project that Alice undertook was more complex than the spreadsheet projects her colleagues had previously designed. Do you think there would be a level of complexity beyond which an end-user would be unable to develop an application? In other words, at one point do you think the professional staff at central data processing muxt play a major role in the development of a project?
12. Every computer project must have a payoff to the organization. What was the payoff with Alice's project?
13. Do you think an end-user project must eventually have an economic payoff to the user in lower costs, higher revenue, greater profits, or some combination of these?
14. While some software vendors claim that end-users need no training to use their software, there is seldom any truth to this statement. Not only is it necessary to understand how to use the hardware, but it is necessary to learn how to use

the software. And in some applications, such as the one Alice developed, the end-user must learn something about the central data processing environment. Since most end-users are primarily business people rather than computer experts, do you think that taking the time to learn how to use these systems and to actually develop applications is a worthwhile use of their time?

WEST SIDE ACCOUNTANTS

Hector Romero decided to squarely face a dilemma he had avoided for some time: to computerize or not. Romero, in his mid-thirties, became a CPA in the early 1970s prior to
the invention of the microcomputer. In those days, accountants used desk calculators. Romero still did.

When he finished his schooling, Romero worked a few years for a large CPA firm located in midtown Manhattan.   Romero grew tired of being a small fish in a big pond, however, and struck out on his own, opening a one-man office on the Upper West Side. He wanted greater independence in terms of hours (which would be long in any case) and the type of work he accepted, and freedom in personal matters such as dress and lifestyle considerations since he was, after all, the boss.

His business had grown to the point where two other accountants and a clerk-receptionist shared the workload. The office at West Side Accountants was full of desk calculators -- in fact, Romero still used the oversized model that he had used in school. It sat on his desk and he was loath to part with it.

THE SERVICE BUREAU

There was some irony in not having a computer. The bulk of West Side Accountants' work consisted of handling income tax preparation for individuals and small businesses. The completed returns that Romero supplied his clients were done by computer. West Side used one of over a dozen local service bureaus that accepted data coded by hand on preprinted input forms, entered and processed the data using a sophisticated income-tax processing program, and produced completed forms as output. The service bureau took three or four days to handle a return and charged about $50, depending on the complexity of the return and the number of optional schedules that had to be produced. West Side included the service bureau's charges in fees to clients.

So Romero's customers got rather impressive-looking computer-generated income tax returns to file with the federal, state, and city governments. Yet there was no computer in Romero's office. Romero was proud of being able to run a successful small business on his own in Manhattan, and the old calculator on his desk -- which was about half the size of a typewriter -- was a symbol to him of what he'd achieved.

EXPERTISE CLOSE AT HAND

However, a computer store opened right next door. Romero had to push aside the crepe paper streamers for the store's grand opening just to get to his office. Day after day as he came to work, there were computers flashing various displays provocatively through the windows. He ignored them all.

But then one day Sylvia Best, who turned out to be a salesperson from the computer store, was sitting in Romero's office for a tax-planning appointment. As she spoke, Romero wrote down the various figures she gave and, every now and then, thrashed furiously at his calculator, which noisily printed a result that he then studied.

"You know," Best said, after watching Romero work this way for several minutes, "a computer about the same size as that box could do it a lot better."

Romero, taken aback, looked up. "Not *better*," he said. "*Faster*."

"Well, I'm not so sure," Best said. "You just did a lot of calculations to see if income-averaging made sense for me. With a computer program that handled such matters, you would only have had to enter the income figures for the five years, and the program would have done everything else."

"Would it have done anything I didn't do?" Romero asked. "I got the result, didn't I?"

"Sure, you did, but . . ."

"That's what I meant about faster but not better," Romero said, cutting off the discussion.

OFFICE PROBLEMS

Only minutes after that meeting was finished, however, Sam Clark, one of the accountants who worked for Romero, entered Romero's office with a problem. "When do you want that mailing to go out?" Clark asked. He was referring to a letter explaining some points of the new tax law. Every West Side client was to receive a copy.

"Tomorrow," Romero said. "I've been getting calls every day from people who are worried about the new law. They want to know how it affects them. Besides that, this is a kind of advertising. It helps people to remember that we are still around, and that we're looking out for their best interests."

Clark nodded agreement. "We've got a time problem, though, Hector," Clark said. "To get that letter out, we have to type over 400 labels."

"Just make a photocopy of the ones we used last time," Romero said.

Clark thought a moment. "With a bit of fuss we probably *could* find a copy shop that would be able to photocopy onto perforated labels. But that won't solve our problem, Hector. That master set of addresses is hopelessly out of date. There are people listed on it who haven't been in this office for years. Some of them are probably dead. And we have new customers who aren't listed at all."

"What do you propose?" Romero asked.

"For now, I suggest that someone sit down for a couple of days and get our master client list in order. And for the future, I suggest that we get a computer."

"I just heard that a few minutes ago," Romero remarked.

"There's nothing easier than printing mailing lists with a computer," Clark went on. "They did it in the last office where I worked. And you can also use the computer to keep the list up to date. For that matter, we could have used a word processing program to do the letter itself."

"O.K., O.K.," Romero said. "I suggest that you and I have a meeting with Sylvia Best from that computer store next door. The time has come!"

A PROPOSED SYSTEM

The next day Romero and Clark visited the store. At least ten different computers were turned on and operating, doing such things as rotating complex geometrical forms on screens that displayed the shapes as crisply as if they were professional photographs. Since this all seemed somewhat different from what West Side Accountants had in mind, as well as confusing, Romero and Clark spoke with Best at her desk in the rear of the store, away from the machines.

Sam Clark described the problem with the mailing list.

"How often do you send out letters like that?" Best asked.

"Every year or so," Romero said. "When the tax laws change significantly."

"Well, Sam is right that a word processing program with a mail-merge feature could do both the letters and the mailing lists quite nicely. And we could find you a file manager program that would be easy to use."

"Why would we want a file manager?" Romero asked.

"To keep an up-to-date address list of your clients."

"But I don't know anything about programs," Romero said. "I have so much work to do that I can't spend much time learning about them, either."

"The clerk who runs your office could handle the file manager program. And does he or she type letters and bills?"

"Yes."

"Using a word processing program is easier than typing," Best said. "Now, about those bills -- would you like a program to prepare them as well?"

"Would we!" said Romero. "It's become a problem lately. I mean, we're good accountants, but we're not a collection agency and do not keep terribly close track of who is behind in paying us."

"That's partly because we're at fault ourselves," Clark added. "We sometimes don't send out a bill until two weeks or more after a service is rendered, simply because we're so bogged down with other things to do. So we're never really sure when to start counting the 30 days off until we send a reminder."

"Sam, this sort of problem is common with small businesses. People are too busy doing whatever it is that the business *does* to send bills and reminders efficiently. Does everyone at West Side agree that a computer could help with these administrative tasks?"

"Yes," Romero said. "I knew this was coming," he added.

"Here's my suggestion," Best said. "I have a microcomputer system in mind that would cost under $3000 for hardware and software -- that is, for the computer itself, including a printer, a program to handle your billing, and a word processing program for letters and mailing lists. I can show you the system I mean and calculate the price more exactly."

"But how would we know how to use any of it?" Romero asked.

"I'll show you. We include training sessions with the sale. And when questions come up after the sessions -- and they will -- you know where to find me."

"You didn't say anything about putting a computer on my desk," Romero commented.

"That's right," Best said. "I think your most critical areas to begin with are in record keeping so that you know who your clients are in the first place, and in setting up an efficient billing system. Once you've mastered that, then we can go on to more exotic possibilities. I would like to put a computer on your desk, Hector, with a spreadsheet program that would help you enormously in figuring out deductions and various what if' questions to handle your clients' finances. But let's wait a few months.

If we try to do it all at once, it won't work."

"Tell me," Clark asked, "isn't there some way we could use a computer so that we didn't have to fill out all those forms that we send to the service bureau?"

Best hadn't heard about the service bureau arrangement, and she listened closely while Clark and Romero described it.

"The service bureau probably uses large minicomputers or mainframes -- the largest type -- and quite a complicated program," Best said. "An inexpensive microcomputer system would not be able to offer that processing power. For now, I would stick with your service bureau arrangement, since it works. When you get confident with the computer, we can figure out how to send the data to the service bureau without using any forms at all."

QUESTIONS

1. If you ran West Side Accountants, would you computerize at this point in time?
2. How would West Side's clients benefit from the computer system that Best proposes?
3. It seems clear that the computer billing system would favorably affect West Side's profitability. But how about having that up-to-date list of clients on a computer file -- in what ways might this ultimately make West Side more profitable?
4. Best proposes starting with billing, a client file, and word processing. Why doesn't she suggest replacing Romero's calculator?
5. It is often true that word processing programs have been responsible for newcomers to microcomputers developing a sense of enthusiasm for using their machines. What type of program is likely to have this affect on Romero?
6. Do you agree that it is better not to disturb the working service bureau arrangement until West Side has become familiar with using computers? Or is Best being too conservative in her approach?
7. Best does not suggest preparing the actual tax forms by computer right in the West Side office, even for some future point in time. Why not?
8. In addition to hardware and software, Best is offering a commodity to West Side that it needs very badly. What is it?

SECTION 2

COMPUTER HARDWARE AND SOFTWARE

The cases in this section take a closer look at how computers work and how they are used. Business professionals do not need to understand hardware and software at a highly detailed level. But to use the computer in unanticipated ways, or to become involved in the design of a computer information system, business professionals need to have a general understanding of data entry and storage, how the CPU processes data, and alternative output choices.

The first case in this section, Miller Pharmaceutical, takes a look at the role of microcomputers, minicomputers, and mainframes in a large corporation that faces increasing competition. Sunbelt Airlines, the subject of the second case, wants to computerize its reservation system; the focus here is on data entry and on data handling within the computer. The third case, Hello Graphics, deals with general hardware and software concepts, particularly those involving microcomputers.

MILLER PHARMACEUTICAL

Miller Pharmaceutical, one of the largest ethical drug manufacturers in the world, has just gone through a management upheaval. Jere Hobson, president of the company for the last 12 years, recently took early retirement. Some felt that he was under great pressure to do so. In his place came a much younger and more aggressive manager. Tom Rogers, 35 years old, had been with the company for only five years. But as product line manager, and then as vice-president of marketing, he had distinguished himself as the kind of person that Miller would need to help it through the troubled times ahead.

For the last decade or more Miller had relied on several patents that gave it monopoly positions in segments of the pharmaceutical market. Now the patents were beginning to expire, and already one product was being marketed under a generic name by several competing pharmaceutical houses.

In addition to Miller's loss of monopoly power, the drug industry itself was facing pressures on several fronts. First, the pressure to keep hospitalization and drug therapy costs down placed the pharmaceutical houses under pressure to keep their own prices and production costs under control. On the second front, competition in the drug market was increasing; many companies saw this as a growth field because of the aging population. And on a third front, some recent mergers and acquisitions had produced larger companies that had the wherewithal to undertake major research and development programs, thereby increasing the competition to develop new drugs.

When Rogers first took the chief executive's position he wasted no time in making several changes. For starters, he replaced the director of research and development, the vice-president of production, and the chief information officer. All of these positions, including a new vice-president of marketing, were filled by people brought in from outside firms. To the dismay of many long-term employees, several of them in line for promotions, no internal appointments were made.

LONG-RANGE STRATEGY SESSION

San Juan was a long way from corporate headquarters in St. Louis, but Rogers wanted to take eight of his top people on a week-long retreat to consider the business strategy they would follow over the next few years. Although several of Miller's manufacturing plants were in Puerto Rico and another was only 60 miles away in the Dominican Republic, here was a place in which they could meet with few interruptions.

Rogers considered the information system at Miller a critical ingredient in the company's ability to perform in the pharmaceutical marketplace, so he asked George Chen, the new chief information officer, to take part in the strategy session.

Monday morning of their first day was scheduled as a briefing session. Each participant would present the current status of his or her area of responsibility. During the rest of the week the group would explore new goals and objectives and prepare a preliminary roadmap on how to get from where they were to where they wanted to be.

CURRENT STATUS OF MIS

George Chen was the third speaker on Monday. "As you know," he began, "I have only been here for a few months, and am still learning how the information systems at Miller are structured and how they work. But in this brief time I think I have learned enough to be able to share some generalizations with you. As you will see, some of our computing is good but other applications are quite ineffective.

"To give you an overall picture," Chen went on, "we have one mainframe at headquarters in St. Louis and another in Kansas City, our largest production facility in the mainland United States. At each of our six other production facilities, including the ones in Puerto Rico, we have 15 minicomputers. And to our best knowledge we have about 450 microcomputers spread throughout the corporation. To put the information processing operation in perspective, we spend about $25 million, or about 13 percent of the corporate budget, on computing and telecommunications."

Fran Lodge, vice-president of marketing, interrupted. "George could you spend a minute clarifying what you mean by mainframe, mini, and micro? I have heard so much about supercomputers, mainframes, superminis, minis, supermicros, and micros, that I honestly don't know what these terms mean any more."

"Fran, you're not alone. I have trouble with those terms. Since there is no clear dividing mark between these categories, vendors are often inclined to coin a new term or take some liberties with an existing category to give the impression that their new computers stand out from the crowd. And the major reason why no clear-cut boundaries exist is that machines are improving every day. First, they can process data faster than their predecessors, and second, they have larger primary memory capacity and can support more secondary storage. So you see, even if the boundaries were agreed upon, they would be changing all the time."

FROM SUPERCOMPUTERS TO MICROS

"But that doesn't answer your question, Fran, it only explains the confusion surrounding this issue. So let me tell you how I deal with it. **Supercomputers** are the largest of the computer family. Their cost may fall in the $100 million category, they process data faster than any other machine, and they can support enormous secondary storage facilities. But at the present time only the largest companies, the government, and especially the military use such machines. In fact they are used more in science and engineering than in business.

"**Mainframes**, like we have, are found in most larger corporations," Chen went on. "In fact the largest Fortune 500 firms often have several. These machines cost in the range of $10 million, have processing speeds faster than minis and micros, may handle hundreds or even thousands of users at remote terminals, and can support data storage for all but the largest business applications.

"For example, one of our mainframes has 5 megabytes of main memory, supports over 350 terminals, and includes secondary storage of 2 Gigabytes or 2 billion bytes of data. And it can access data stored on these disk drives very quickly. Average access time, the time it takes to access the data and present it on the screen, is about 20 milliseconds."

"What about our minis?" Fran asked.

"**Minicomputers** are considered an intermediate-range computer. They can do the kind of processing and handle the amount of secondary storage that might be required at a division or department level in an organization, and in smaller companies they might support all of the data processing needs. And these computers may handle as many as several hundred users accessing the system from remote terminals. To give you another example, one of our minis used for production scheduling supports 100 terminals and has 2 megabytes of main memory and 300 megabytes of disk storage. Access time for data on these disks averages 35 milliseconds.

"The **microcomputers**, on the other hand, are the smallest machines. Micros are self-contained in that the unit includes the keyboard, the central processing unit, one or two floppy disk drives, and in many cases a hard disk drive. A typical micro may have 640 Kilobytes of main memory, a floppy disk drive that can store about 360 Kilobytes on a 5-1/4 inch floppy disk or 1.2 Megabytes on a 3-1/2 inch floppy. Access times for these floppies average about 200 milliseconds. Their hard disks can store in the range of 20 to 40 megabytes with access times in the range of 50 milliseconds.

"When used in the stand-alone mode, micros perform only local data processing functions. Little or no processing that affects more than one person is likely to be done on these machines. But many of the micros in use today are networked together so that a group of micros can share a common hard disk, and in that way share data resources among micro users. In addition, some of these networks provide access to the data stored on minis and mainframes."

"George, do we have this networking capability?" asked Roger.

"No. The previous computing philosophy here at Miller was to keep everything tightly under the control of central data processing. Since networks could weaken that control, the philosophy was to minimize the use of this technology."

"Does this mean that most of our computers don't communicate with each other?" asked Fran.

"Exactly," George said. "But I think we ought to wait until tomorrow to discuss this aspect of the information system, since it's part of the long-range information strategy proposal that I would like to present to you."

HOW THEY ARE USED

Roger interrupted. "George, can you explain how we use these mainframes, minis, and micros?"

"All right," George said. "The corporate mainframe is used mainly for sales order entry and accounting. When a customer places the order, it is entered by order clerks into a terminal. The computer initiates a credit check on the customer, and if the customer's account is current, then the order is added to the sales file. The accounting department uses the mainframe for general ledger accounting. This is the system in which all of the accounting records for the corporation are maintained. Sales amounts are entered, together with expenses, wages, purchases, and taxes. And it is from this general ledger system that we prepare monthly, quarterly, and end-of-year financial statements. We also maintain accounts receivable and accounts payable systems on the mainframe. The accounts receivable system keeps detailed records of the customers who owe us money, and it helps us manage the collection of these accounts. The accounts payable system keeps track of who it is that we owe money to, and automatically notifies us when these bills are due."

"I should add that these mainframes have an 'operating system' which includes software that coordinates the functions performed by the computer hardware, the central processing unit (the computer itself), the input/output units like terminals and printers, and the secondary storage devices, which in our case include disk drives. These operating systems are quite complex and provide the intelligence for the system to coordinate all the requests made by the application software and process jobs in either the batch or on-line mode. When the on-line mode is used, the data are processed instantly by the computer and the user has access to the data in the central database. We use on-line computing for sales order entry and all our accounting functions. So when an accounting clerk needs to update a customer's account to reflect a payment, the customer's record can be accessed by that clerk instantly. But these operating systems also support 'batch' processing in which data are processed in groups. We use this approach for producing monthly statements, which are sent to our customers. These statements summarize the balance due in the customer's accounts. And we also use batch processing to produce many of the Management Information System (MIS) reports that are sent to the staff every week.

"The minis are primarily used at the manufacturing division level," George continued. "They cost in the range of $100,000, and are used to process local payrolls and to maintain inventory and production scheduling data for the plant. So if we wanted to know how much inventory of a particular stock unit we had in the South Carolina plant, we could have someone query that mini and access the inventory database. We could also learn from those minis when production runs were scheduled and how many items were to be produced on a particular run. And like the mainframes, the minis have operating systems that support both on-line and batch processing.

"While the use of the mainframes and minis has been carefully managed and controlled by the central data processing department, the use of micros has not. They have sprouted up throughout the organization whenever a particular individual or group felt that it could justify buying them from its budget. They are used by secretaries and administrative assistants for word processing. Some of the accountants and finance staff use them to build spreadsheets, and a very few individuals build their own applications like databases and project management on the micros."

Fran interrupted. "George, I hope you plan to talk about our micro policy in depth tomorrow. From what I can tell when I visit other organizations, the micro is rapidly becoming the link to the corporate information system, and if we don't develop micro networks and then support some access from those networks to the minis and mainframes, I'm afraid we'll miss an oportunity to use our information resources to best advantage."

"I will try to give this the time it deserves," was George's reply.

QUESTIONS

1. Why is there some confusion over the categorization of computers?
2. Which computer category processes data the fastest? Which category processes data the slowest? Give examples.
3. What type of computer supports the most secondary storage? . Which type supports the least?

4. How would you compare a microcomputer and a minicomputer?
5. Compare the cost of a mainframe and mini.
6. Go to the library and find a computer periodical such as *PC, PC Week*, or *Byte*. Find an advertisement for a micro. The speed of micros is measured in microseconds. Is the speed listed for the micro you found? Does the micro use floppy disks? Is a hard disk supplied as standard equipment or is it an option? How much does the micro cost? If it is an option, how much does the hard disk cost?
7. What applications are run on Miller's mainframe?
8. What is the purpose of a general ledger application? Account receivable? Do you think you need an on-line system for these applications?
9. What is the difference between on-line and batch processing? Give examples of each from the case.
10. Why wouldn't you expect to find any of a corporation's larger applications (applications used by many individuals) on a stand-alone micro?
11. In a large corporation, such as Miller Pharmaceutical, do you think all decisions for computer purchases and computer applications should be made by a centralized data processing group located at corporate headquarters, or do you think some decisions might be left to the local divisions and even local work groups?
12. How does this case suggest that it is not just the isolated pieces of hardware and software in a system that are important, but the way in which they work together to meet the needs of users?

SUNBELT AIRLINES

Sunbelt Airlines is a small commuter airline serving the Miami, Palm Beach, Orlando, and Tampa-St. Petersburg markets. The fleet consists of nine British Islander planes, each with a capacity of nine passengers and a pilot.

Until now the reservation system was manual. To make a reservation, customers called an 800 number, which connected them with the reservation desk at company headquarters in Miami. The reservation clerk would take the request, see if space was available, and if it was, enter the reservation into the reservation log.

NEW OPPORTUNITIES

With several recent mergers and acquisitions, the larger trunk airlines cut back on service between the cities that Sunbelt served as well as service to other cities in Florida. Will Garnet, president of Sunbelt, thought this was an excellent opportunity for the airline to expand. And he had the financial backing of several investors. They too saw an opportunity for a regional airline whose operating costs could be kept in line with ticket revenues.

PROPOSAL FOR A NEW SYSTEM

In anticipation of this move, Will asked Guy Stearns, the vice-president of operations, to look into a computer reservation system.

Guy began by contacting several computer companies. Reserve Computing was the first to make a presentation. Fay Henson arrived with brochures and a slide presentation. "Where should I begin?" she asked.

"First you might give us some background about your company," Guy responded.

"All right. We've been in the computer business for almost ten years and have specialized in reservation systems for hotels, restaurants, auto rental agencies, and small airlines. Our customers range from a single-location 50-room motel to a chain of ten car rental agencies. And we have installed these systems at locations you would probably recognize." She went on to name a few. "And we're currently installing an airline reservation system for another small commuter airline in Texas. I'm sure you know them too, Panhandle Flyways."

"Can you describe that system for us?" Will asked.

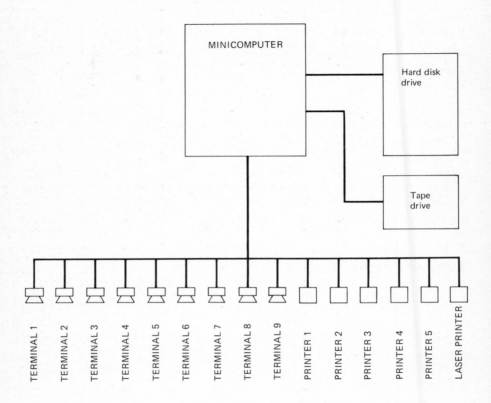

Figure 1. The system will support secodary storage devices, 9 reservation terminals, 5 draft quality printers, and one laser printer.

"In fact, I brought some slides which show exactly how their system works." Fay loaded her slide tray into the projector and dimmed the lights for the first slide (Figure 1).

"The hardware in this system includes a minicomputer with two megabytes of main memory, a hard disk with 200 megabytes of secondary storage, a tape drive for back-up storage, nine terminals to be used by the reservation clerks and the office personnel, five draft quality printers, and one laser printer used for letter quality hard copy.

"When data are stored in the primary memory of the CPU and when they are stored on hard disk or tape," Fay continued, "the data are stored in a binary format. The computer keeps this binary data in bit cells. A group of eight bit cells is called a **byte**, and it takes a byte to store a number, letter, or special character. So when we say that primary memory has the capacity to store two megabytes of data and programs this means that it can store two million bytes or characters at a time.

Figure 2. The on-line system will collect passenger reservation data.

And our hard disk can store 200 million bytes of data, or the equivalent of over 500 paperback books.

"It takes one byte to store a letter or number, and our newest computer processes four bytes at a time. This is referred to as 32-bit computer, and the benefit to you is that the response time of the computer is faster. Just as a four-lane highway can 'process' more cars at any point in time than a two-lane highway can process, a 32-bit computer can process more data at one time than a 16-bit computer can process. This means that your reservation people won't have to wait long when they have to request data or when entering a reservation. Some of our competitors are selling 16-bit systems, so you have to be careful on this point.

"Let's move over to the functions of the system. We'll first look at the data that go into the system. This slide shows the data reservation screen (Figure 2). The screen requires the user to enter the customer's name, address, telephone number, flight number, date, method of payment, and credit card number. We refer to each of these categories as a data **field**. So in this case we have a name field, an address field, a telephone number field, and so on. A **record** is a collection of related fields, so together these field make up what we refer to as a Personal Reservation Record (PRR).

"A **file** is a collection of logically related records," Fay went on, "so the collection of PRRs is what we refer to as the PRR file.

"Now I should point out that ours is an on-line system. **On-line** refers to the fact that the terminals are in direct contact with the CPU. In addition our system is also in direct contact with the PRR file. This means that whenever a reservation is made, the file is updated immediately, so if another reservation clerk accesses the same file a few moments later, that clerk would find that the seat that was just requested is no longer available.

"This on-line feature is the result of sophisticated system software called the **operating system**. It manages the resources of the computer, including the disk storage system, and in addition oversees the use of the system so that as many as 30 remote terminals can be tied to the minicomputer at once. Some refer to this as a multiuser system. Meanwhile, users at each of these terminals could, if they wanted to, be performing different tasks, and as a result this is also called a multitasking system. As you can see the operating system in this computer is busy with all the record keeping necessary to allow many users to share the system simultaneously without interfering with each other's needs."

AUTOMATED DATA ENTRY

"Can I tell you what bothers me about this system?" Will asked.

"Please do."

"It seems that everyone is moving toward some form of automated data entry," Will said. "Supermarkets use bar code scanners to enter product data, utilities use machine-readable reply cards which the customers include with their payment, and even banks rely on their customers to enter their own data through automatic teller machines. But here you are trying to sell me a system where we have to have clerks sit in front of a terminal and enter data that they receive from the customer over the telephone. If we do it this way our data entry costs will be as high as the manual system were using now. Where do we get any benefits by buying your system?"

"If there were a better way of entering data we would have it," Fay said. "But reservations can't be entered that way. There have been no breakthroughs in the field of source data automation to make this economically feasible. You will be in the same boat as everyone else in the reservation business, I'm afraid. Entries will have to be manual."

QUESTIONS

1. Why would it be disadvantageous for Sunbelt to continue using its current reservation methods?
2. Raw data are the data that are entered into the computer. Give an example of raw data in the reservation system.
3. How many bits are in a byte? How many bytes are in a megabyte?
4. What factors did Fay mention when describing the size of the computer system? What is the difference between machines of different sizes?
5. What is a data field? Identify the fields in the reservation system.
6. Describe the PPR.

7. What is a file?
8. Why is the system which Faye is recommending called an on-line system? What is a multiuser, multitasking, on-line system?
9. What does an operating system do? Give two examples of the functions performed by an operating system.
10. Describe a system you have seen which uses source data automation.
11. Why do you think it would be difficult to use source data automation in this application? Do you think that customers need to interact with a reservation agent? Would it be possible to offer two methods of data entry, one in which the customer could use automated methods, and the other in which a reservation clerk would be used when the customer needed help? What benefits and disadvantges would you expect with such a system?
12. Suppose a second vendor made a presentation and in response to Will's concern about data entry costs suggested that they look into the use of touch-tone phones. Customers would receive directions over the phone and respond by pressing the buttons on their phone. Do you think this suggestion is worth exploring? Could it work?
13. If you had to make a recommendation to Will once several vendors had made their presentations, what characteristics of the hardware and software would be most important to you? Why?
14. If data entry costs will be as high with the new system as they are with the manual system, how can Will justify spending the money for a new system?
15. How would you proceed at this point? What would be you next step?

HELLO GRAPHICS

Hello Graphics, a greeting card manufacturer located in upstate New York, was started 12 years ago by Stuart Fonfa. Since that time the company has grown rapidly, and in addition to its very successful line of greeting cards Hello now has a line of stylish stationery, aprons, tote bags, and umbrellas.

Five years ago, in response to overwhelming paperwork and lack of control, Hello purchased its first computer, an IBM PC. According to Fonfa, that PC and another purchased a few years later helped considerably.

When Fonfa purchased that first computer he had a lot to learn. He learned about programs, central processing units, data entry, data output, and secondary storage.

PROGRAMS

First he learned that computers can perform such simple steps as adding, subtracting, multiplying, dividing, and making logical comparisons. Because computers can only perform these simple operations -- but perform them very fast -- a **program** must be written that breaks a processing task into a series of these simple steps for the machine to follow.

CENTRAL PROCESSING UNIT

The **central processing unit (CPU)** includes a primary storage area -- sometimes called **main memory** -- and is responsible for temporarily storing data and programs while they are being processed. The CPU also includes an **arithmetic/logic unit (ALU)**, which is reponsible for performing the real work including adding, subtracting, multiplying, dividing, and making logical comparisons.

Programs are made up of the step-by-step instructions used to solve a processing problem in a sequence and format that the computer understands. And because the ALU can only add, multiply, divide, subtract, and make logical comparisons, the program must break all processing tasks into these simple steps.

While the CPU does the processing, there are three other functions performed in even the simplest microcomputer. They include data entry, data output, and secondary storage.

DATA ENTRY AND DATA OUTPUT

Data entry refers to the entry of data into the computer system. Usually this is accomplished through a keyboard. **Data output**, the results of the processing fuction, usually appears on the screen of the microcomputer or is printed on paper using a printer.

PRIMARY AND SECONDARY STORAGE

Primary storage is limited in size, expensive, and volatile. It is volatile because when the computer is turned off the data and programs are lost. More permanent storage, **secondary storage**, occurs on disk. Three types of disk are common with micros. A **floppy disk**, so named because the disk is flexible, is available in two configuarations, a 5-1/4 inch and 3-1/2 inch version. They are the least expensive storage medium. A **hard disk**, so named because it is built on a rigid aluminum platter, is capable of storing up to 20 times the data stored on a floppy disk and can also retrieve data in much less time. **Optical disks** are relatively new storage media, and can store very large quantities of data, but suffer from slower access times than hard disks. Unlike the data on a hard or floppy disk, the data on an optical disk can not be erased and rewritten.

8-,16-, AND 32-BIT MACHINES

The size of a computer is measured by the size of its main memeory. Many machines have the capacity to temporarily store 640 kilobytes of data. But computers are also measured by the number of bits that can be stored in one storage location. This also represents the number of bits that can be processed at once. Three sizes are common: 8, 16, and 32. An 8-bit computer can process 8 bits of data at a time, a 16-bit computer can process 16 bits at a time, and a 32-bit computer can process 32 bits at a time. As a rule, the more data that can be stored in a storage location and processed at a time, the faster and more powerful is the machine. And faster machines are needed in business when complex software must be processed by the machine, when a high volume of data must be processed, or when high quality graphics are demanded.

OPERATING SYSTEMS

Software is a collection of programs. Two types of software are used with a computer. **Application software** is the software that directs the computer to perform user-related tasks like accounting or reservations. **System software** is the collection of programs that manage the resources of the computer system and provide supporting functions for application programs. One category of system software is the **operating system**. It coordinates the functions performed by the computer hardware -- including the CPU, input/output units, and secondary storage devices.

CURRENT COMPUTERS

The first computer Fonfa purchased in 1984, an IBM PC, was used for billing, accounts receivable, and inventory control. He purchased the original IBM PC, which was introduced in August 1981. It was an 8-bit machine with 256 KB of main memory, and with two 5-1/2 inch floppy drives capable of storing 135 KB of data and programs on a floppy disk.

When Fonfa was asked how Hello Graphics benefited from this computer he was quick to respond that customers were now billed immediately upon shipment of their goods, not a week or two later. In addition, the accounts receivable system provided more control over the balances that customers owed the company. Billing immediately and controlling receivables brought cash into the company faster and reduced Hello's need to borrow from local banks. And lower interest charges meant higher profits.

In 1987 Hello purchased two more PCs. Both were used in the office for word processing.

A NEW COMPUTER

Fonfa is now shopping for two new computers. He will use one himself for financial analysis, and plans to develop his own applications using spreadsheet software. The other will be used by the marketing group for desktop publishing. They plan to use the system to produce promotional literature and to experiment with the process of designing and storing their card designs on the system.

In desktop publishing the computer is used to produce hard copy similar in quality to that produced by a commercial printing house. Specialized desktop hardware and software provide the means by which text and images can be entered into a computer and processed. The software can be used to combine the text and images into a format that can even resemble that of a newspaper.

The computer used to support desktop publishing must have the capability to store, process, and display images, graphics, and illustrations. This can require both a considerable amount of storage space and high processing speeds.

Fonfa has narrowed his search for the two computers to the IBM Personal System/2 product line. The line includes four models: models 30, 50, 60, and 80.

Model 30 uses a 8086 processor, and is an 8-bit machine with 640 KB of main memory (a **KB** or **kilobyte** is equal to about one thousand bytes or characters of data that can be stored). It also includes a 3-1/2 inch diskette with a capacity of 720 KB, and a 20-MB hard disk (an **MB** or **megabyte** is equal to about one million bytes or characters of data).

Models 50 and 60 use a 80286 processor, are 16-bit machines, and have 1 MB (expandable to 15 MB) of main memory. These models also include a 3-1/2 inch diskette with a capacity to store 1.44 MB of data and a 44- or 70-MB hard disk.

Model 80 uses a 80386 processor, is a 32-bit machine, and has up to 2 MB of main memory. It includes a 1.44 MB 3-1/2 inch diskette and a choice of a 44-, 70-, or 115-MB hard drive. In its maximum configuration, the model 80 can support 230 MB of hard disk storage.

An optical storage system can be used with all models. The system called a **WORM** -- an acronym for Write Once Read Many times -- has the capacity to store 200 MB of data and programs. Data, however, can only be written on the disk once. Thereafter the data can be read many times, but the original data on the disk cannot be erased or changed.

Model 30 uses a PC DOS 3.3 operating system, while the other machines are also capable of using the more powerful Operating System/2 (OS/2). The OS/2 will support multitasking, in which several programs can be run at once. So the computer can receive and store electronic mail, mainframe data, or whatever, while the user is busy doing something else on the computer.

The graphics capabilities of the models 50, 60, and 80 are what IBM has called "dazzling." In the color mode as many as 256 colors can be painted on the screen at once. And the **resolution**, measured by the number of dots or **pixels** across one line on the screen and the total number of lines, provides high-quality images. These models are well suited for producing quality brochures and newsletters.

In addition to a computer, desktop publishing will require a digitizer or optical scanner, a device that converts a photo or any image, even a printed page, into a form which can be processed by the CPU, stored on disk and presented on the screen. When these images are entered into the optical scanner, it takes about 10 to 45 seconds to convert a standard 8.5 X 11-inch page into digital information. And these scanners are really necessary in desktop publishing since many applications require the integration of text and images on a single page of output. The scanner provides a simple and economical way to enter these images. Finally, a Laser printer is needed to produce the high-quality hard copy output.

QUESTIONS

1. What is a microcomputer?
2. Describe the purpose of the CPU.
3. What is the ALU?
4. What is the difference between main memory and secondary storage?
5. Desribe the differences between floppy disks and hard disks.
6. Give an example of data input and output for the type of spreadsheet applications which Fonfa has in mind.
7. What is meant when a computer is described as a 32-bit machine?
8. Is the computer that uses an 80386 processor classified as a 32- or 16-bit machine? How is the computer that uses an 8086 processor classified?
9. Describe the IBM PS/2 model 50.
10. Describe the IBM PS/2 models 60 and 70.
12. Desribe the IBM PS/2 model 80.
13. What is the advantage of using an optical drive with these machines? What are the disadvantages?
14. What is multitasking, and which machine supports this feature?
15. What application software did Fonfa purchase with his first machine? Was it successful? Explain.
16. For what applications are the new machines needed?
17. What machine would you consider to be appropriate for the spreadsheet applications?
18. What is desktop publishing and why might it be useful at Hello Graphics.
19. What hardware is needed to support desktop publishing? Which machine(s) would be appropriate for the desktop publishing application?
20. Describe the function of an optical scanner.
21. Do you think Fonfa needs a machine capable of multitasking?
22. How would you proceed to select a machine?

SECTION 3

DATA INPUT AND OUTPUT

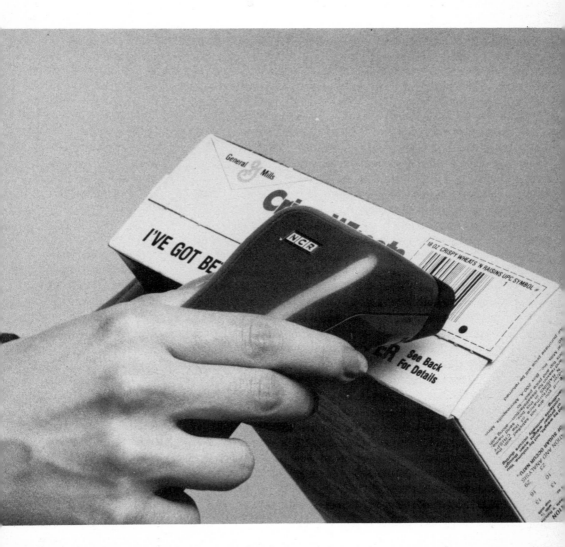

Data are the raw facts that are entered into a computer, such as a person's name, a bank balance, or a cost estimate on a spreadsheet. Getting data into a computer accurately and efficiently is a goal of any computer information system, and particularly of transaction systems, which handle large volumes of data. A number of today's data entry alternatives are illustrated by the cases in this section.

The output from a computer information system is the point at which most business professionals interface with the system. To constitute an effective aid to the decision-making process, output should be timely, reliable, and easy to understand. This is sometimes easier said than done, as will be seen.

Three cases concerning data input and output are presented in this section. The first, Baker & Young, presents a distribution firm that wants to obtain a strategic edge over competitors by taking advantage of technological developments in data entry methods; specifically, they are interested in a computer-based self-ordering system. Hoosier Gourmet, the foods distributor of the second case, is saddled with an ineffective inventory control system, and debates the ability of source data automation to solve its problems. The third case, State Welfare Department, presents alternatives for streamlining data input and output methods in a government setting.

BAKER & YOUNG

Baker & Young is a national distributor of industrial machinery and accessories. The firm carries a range of manufacturing equipment and supplies including drill presses, electric motors, workbenches, precision measuring equipment, and fasteners.

Twice each year Baker & Young mails 5000 catalogs to its customers. The current catalog is over 300 pages long and includes some 20,000 items.

THE ORDER ENTRY PROCESS

Orders are placed in one of three ways. Most customers call through an 800 number; others send an order through the mail; and some place orders through independent sales reps that carry the line.

When an order is received, it is written on an order entry form and sent to central data processing, where data entry clerks enter the data using key-to-disk machines. After the data are entered and verified they are saved on disk and later used to update the central order file.

Although this order entry sytem has proven satisfactory in the past, Peter Barbera, vice-president of marketing, feels that technological developments in the computer industry offer the firm the oportunity to upgrade the order entry process and obtain several benefits. These would include a strategic edge over their competitors, lower error rates in the order entry process, a reduction in the cost to process an order, and quicker shipments of customer orders.

At the present time it takes about four working days for an order to get through the system. Since shipping by UPS -- the carrier used to ship most small orders -- takes on the average another three days, customers must wait at least a week for a shipment to arrive. In many situations this is simply too long.

Errors in the data entry process have always been a problem. In the worst case a customer places an order with a rep, the rep calls the order into headquarters, the order taker writes the order on an order form, and the order is entered by data entry clerks in the the data entry department. With four people involved, there are many opportunities for order numbers, quantities, and shipping instructions to be relayed incorrectly.

A COMPUTER-BASED SELF-ORDERING SYSTEM

While reading an article in a marketing journal about a medical products distributor, Barbera suddenly realized that a similar system could work for Baker & Young. The medical products distributor used its system not only to keep track of a complex array of 120,000 products but also to attract and hold onto its customers. They called their system a computer-based self-ordering sytem.

Customers who use this self-ordering system enter order data including catalog numbers, descriptions, and quanitites, into their own computer terminals. When they finish they send the order over the telephone network directly into the medical product company's central computer. This service has been so successful that the medical products distributor claims that nearly half of its customers -- hospitals and clinics -- enter their orders this way. The benefit is that customers enter the orders themselves, verify that the data are correct, and send the data directly into the corporate computer.

BAR CODES AND OPTICAL WANDS

The next morning Barbera walked into Ed Scully's office. He told Scully, the MIS manager, about the article he had read. Scully showed some interest but did not share Barbera's enthusiasm.

"I like that approach, Peter, but let me tell you about another one I discovered a few months ago. One of our competitors is thinking of developing a system that uses bar codes in their catalog. Here's how their system will work. The catalog will include a bar code printed next to each item description. This bar code, like the ones you see on the items we buy at the supermarket, will have a unique set of lines for each product in the catalog. In addition to this bar code the company will also issue a small hand-held computer and optical wand to its customers. When customers want to place an order, they run the optical wand over the bar code, enter the number of units desired with the small calculator-like keyboard, and then proceed to the next item they need. Once they have entered all this data, they can review it on the screen, and when they are sure that the data are O.K. they call an 800 number, press the send button on the hand-held deveice, and transmit the order over the telephone network to the distributor's central computer. Pretty neat, I think!"

Peter and Ed discussed both alternatives. Although they disagreed about which approach would best meet their needs, they did agree that they must move toward source data entry if not to source data automation.

QUESTIONS

1. Define the problem presented in this case.
2. How are orders currently entered at Baker & Young?
3. Describe how errors enter into the current system.
4. What would be the consequences, five to ten years from now, if the company were to stay with its present sales order entry system?
5. How do you think an automated sales order entry system at Baker & Young would affect sales order processing costs?
6. How would an automated system affect delivery of goods to customers?
7. Describe the system that Barbera read about.
8. How did the system work that Scully described?
9. What additional equipment would be needed if Barbera's method is chosen? What equipment would be needed if Scully's method is chosen?
10. "Customers should not be allowed access to Baker & Young's computer. The system would then be too accessible to unauthorized users." Do you agree with this statement? Justify your answer.
11. Do you think an automated sytem like the one described by Barbera or Scully would eliminate all data entry errors? Explain.
12. Would you expect all of Baker & Young's customers to use this system? Would they all have to use the system to make it a success?
13. Do you think customers would prefer Barbera's or Scully's system?
14. If you were the MIS manager, which method would you prefer?

HOOSIER GOURMET

Hoosier Gourmet is a distributor of imported gourmet and specialty foods serving retail grocery and gourmet food stores in the Midwest. Although Hoosier has used computers for many years, one of their systems -- inventory control -- has never worked well.

The problem is that the balances for items maintained in inventory are seldom accurate. When Carl Hoyt, one of seven sales reps, used his terminal last week to see if there was enough stock to meet a customer's order, the balance reported on the screen was more than enough to meet the order; but when the order was sent to the warehouse, three out of the fifteen items ordered were out of stock and four were short of the amount needed.

LOST CUSTOMERS

Hoyt has always been critical of the system. He has complained that he loses customers because of it. He tells them the items are in stock, but then they don't receive delivery. The result, reasonably enough, is that they go to competitors who can make good on their promises.

At a recent meeting Hoyt told the manager of distribution that the company should get another computer or it would continue to lose customers.

The head of marketing, Paula Morrissy, thought that a new computer might not be necessary, but that new inventory software should be used. Her feeling was that Hoosier needed better methods and procedures to do the job properly.

But it wasn't just Hoyt and Morrissy that had an opinion. Larry Long, hired three years before to oversee the computer operations at Hoosier, was particularly frustrated by this problem and by his powerlessness to do anything about it.

Long explained that there are several times during the month, especially during holiday periods, when a crunch of orders occurs. At these times the stockroom is in chaos. Orders to be shipped are stacked everywhere, and the staff is clearly overworked. Since it is not good policy to delay shipments and leave customers with empty shelves, the goal in the stockroom is to get the orders out as soon as possible. Often this means rushing orders out the back door, and more often than not it is the inventory record-keeping process that suffers. Although the stockroom personnel deny Long's acusation, he is certain that in the rush to get orders out, stock depletions are entered incorrectly into the terminals -- or worse, not entered at all.

SOURCE DATA AUTOMATION

Last week the president of Hoosier, Ed Lambert, suggested that Long look into the use of bar codes for identifying stock. "Why can't we put bar code labels, like the ones used on most grocery items, on all our containers? Then, whenever items are added or withdrawn from stock, the bar code would be read much like it is read at the supermarket checkout counter. Once it is read, the product code can be sent to our computer and the inventory record automatically updated. Larry, by automating the data entry process I'm sure we'll solve a lot of our problems. Can you look into this and send me a report in a few days?"

Long was not convinced that using bar codes would end all of Hoosier's inventory problems -- source data automation was not always the answer -- but in this case he did think an improvement could be made.

Long found that new hardware and software needed to be purchased. First, they had to have a printer capable of printing bar code labels. Since these labels would be affixed to every box that the receiving department received, he concluded that they had to have the capacity to print over 3000 bar codes each day. They could choose either a dot matrix, ink jet, or laser printer, but at the volume they needed a laser printer was probably the best choice.

In addition to the printer they needed laser wands at several locations in the receiving, inventory, and shipping areas so that it would be possible to record the movement of goods either in or out of stock. These wands would be capable of reading the lines of various thickness that make up a bar code.

Finally, they needed bar code software. This software would be capable of managing the process of reading the bar code label, converting the bar code into a computer useable format, and maintaining a lookup table in the database so that the bar code for a particular inventory item could be associated with its product ID number. Once the product ID is determined the database could be updated.

After collecting this information, Long summarized his findings in a report. When he received it, Lambert called a meeting that included Hoyt and Morrissy.

At the meeting Hoyt felt the bar code project was worth a try, but Morrissy, on the other hand, was convinced that this was a case of looking in the wrong direction to solve a problem. "This isn't a computer problem," she insisted, "it's a management problem! If your stockroom personnel don't take the time to follow current procedures, what makes you think they will do so after we spend $20,000 on a new system?"

QUESTIONS

1. What is the problem?
2. Do Lambert, Hoyt, and Morrissy agree on the cause of the problem? If not, explain their differing points of view.
3. What is source data automation?
4. Explain how bar codes work in a supermarket.
5. How would bar codes work at Hoosier?
6. What hardware and software would be needed to handle bar codes?
7. What is the function of the software?
8. Will bar coding solve Hoosier's problem?
9. If you were Lambert, what do you think your next step would be?

STATE WELFARE

The memo received from the governor's office was short and to the point: the budget increase requested by the State Department of Welfare was not approved. Instead, funding for the administrative activities of the department would be the same as last year.

Nancy Brooks, director of the agency, called a meeting of department heads and asked them to consider ways in which expenses could be contained. Two proposals she received from the accounting department focused on the same issue -- welfare check paperwork.

THE PRESENT SYSTEM

To prepare welfare checks the present computer system accesses the recipient database to determine those eligible to receive a check, the amount of each check, and the recipient's address. Then the check is printed and mailed. During this process several forms and controls are used to insure that only authorized payments are made.

AUTOMATIC PAYMENT PROPOSAL

The report that Peter Brown re-submitted to Nancy was actually an old proposal. Now, however, he felt its time had come. In the memo to her he explained that the current system was costly from several different points of view. First, the administrative costs of mailing the checks -- including the costs of security and control -- were high. Second, the welfare department actually had little control over the delivery of the check to the authorized recipient. They knew that, as a result, checks were often cashed by unauthorized people. "While we can't completely eliminate fraud and theft," Peter explained, "I think we should consider automating the process. I know it will help solve this problem."

He went on to say that the computer would continue to store data about each welfare recipient and when payment was due. Recipients would be issued plastic identification cards much like a credit card. On this card would be personal data encoded on a magnetic strip and a photo ID.

Participating banks would then be issued card readers that would be used to read the data encoded on the card. When the welfare recipient requested payment, the teller would then verify the identity of the person using the photo, and insert the card into the reader. The data from the card would be sent to the central computer at the welfare department, where the request for payment would be processed. If the computer determines that payment can be made, then a message will be returned to the teller's card reader authorizing the transaction and specifying the amount to be paid. After the transaction is completed, the teller will confirm payment on the card reader and an electronic transfer of funds will be initiated by the central welfare computer to the bank's account.

Peter emphasized that the data on welfare recipients were already in the computer system, and to mail checks every month in this age of electronic funds transfer was to cling to manual output methods. "Now," he concluded, "is the time to begin an overdue effort to use source data automation methods."

EQUIPMENT UPGRADE PROPOSAL

Berny Chernovick, also employed in the accounting department, had a different view of how the welfare department could be made more efficient. Berny's proposal suggested the replacement of equipment which was now 15 years old. He recommended the purchase of new high-speed laser printers for printing checks, envelopes, and reports. Berny insisted that outdated equipment was responsible for administrative waste.

QUESTIONS

1. Describe the current system used to send welfare checks.
2. What is the output from the current system?
3. Describe Peter Brown's proposal.
4. What is electronic funds transfer?
5 What is the output in Brown's proposed system?
6. How would source data automation be used in this proposal?
7. Do you think a bank would prefer to process a welfare check under the present system or under the proposed system?
8. How was source data automation used to verify the welfare recipient? Could a photo ID system be used with the current system to verify the authenticity of the welfare recipient?
9. What input to the bank's computer system would occur as a result of Brown's proposed welfare check transaction?
10. Describe the proposal submitted by Chernovic. Does it involve source data automation?

11. The card reader used by the teller would rely on screen output. Would you recommend voice output instead? Explain.
12. Rather than a card reader, do you think it would be preferable to use a keyboard? Justify your answer.
13. Which proposal requires the most changes to the methods and procedures required by the bank to make payment? Explain.
14. Compare the benefits and disadvantages of both proposals.
15. What would be your next step?

SECTION 4

DATA STORAGE
AND
RETRIEVAL

Once data are input they must be stored; before data or information can be output they must be retrieved. The media and methods used for data storage and retrieval have a pronounced impact on the effectiveness of a computer information system, particularly a transaction system, which processes large quantities of data.

The first case presented here deals with the characteristics of disk storage; Coastal Trucking evaluates a move from using floppy disks to a hard disk in order to speed up its system's sluggish data retrieval times. In the second case, Quik Inc., an overnight delivery service, is interested in gaining a competitive advantage through an on-line customer inquiry system that offers quick access to data. Moving to such a system also entails understanding some of the mechanics of data storage and retrieval on disk.

COASTAL TRUCKING

Joe O'Brien of Coastal Trucking was shopping for a computer. His company, a common carrier that hauled goods along the Atlantic Seaboard from Maine to Pennsylvania, was growing fast. He felt it was time to replace the microcomputer they had been using for accounting and accounts receivable.

Jim Connoly, a salesperson for Data Design, had presented O'Brien with a proposal for a minicomputer system that could support a variety of applications in addition to the general ledger accounting and accounts receivable applications already supported by Coastal's microcomputer. It could also support payroll, customer billing, fleet maintenance, and many other specialized accounting systems such as fuel and road taxes, which, by law, trucking companies were required to pay to states through which they hauled goods. Above all, the proposed system would provide access to several users at once. Now only one can use the microcomputer at a time.

The proposed system is classified as a multiuser, multitasking system. As the vendor explained, a **multiuser system** is one that can support many simultaneous users, each one at a separate terminal. A **multitasking system** allows each of these users to perform different tasks; for example, one might be entering an accounts receivable payment while another is entering general ledger data.

O'Brien is especially concerned about the proposed system's storage methods. The microcomputer that they were then using relied on floppy disks to store data and programs. But O'Brien was unhappy with this approach, for several reasons. First, it often took over 20 seconds just to get data out of the system. The accounting clerks complained that this slowed them down, and since they shared one machine, there was often a backlog of transactions waiting to be entered. Second, the system couldn't accommodate a better accounting system, one that needed more on-line storage. Third, the software they did use was on four disks, and the accounting clerks were constantly changing disks as they moved from one accounting step to the next.

When Jim Connoly returned for a second sales call, O'Brien asked him several questions, including one about the storage system.

A HARD DISK

Connoly explained that the system could be purchased with a hard disk that, depending on the model, could store from 40 to 500 MB. "To give you some perspective," he explained, "your floppies can only store 270 KB of data and programs. So the hard disk stores between 160 to 2000 times as much data and programs! This means all of your programs and data can be stored permanently on the hard disk and you will no longer need to swap floppies as you move between applications. And with this level of storage capacity there will be lots of room to add new applications.

"Access times will also be significantly better. Depending on the drive you select, **access time** -- or the time between the moment a request is made for data and the appearance of the data on the screen -- will be between 15 and 45 milliseconds. A millisecond is a thousandth of a second. Access time with your floppy is about 300 milliseconds, or about ten times longer than the access time possible on a hard disk."

"How is it possible to get access time down this low?" asked O'Brien.

"Hard disks are made of a rigid aluminum platter over which a magnetic oxide or thin-film metallic medium is deposited. Data and programs are recorded magnetically on this layer, much the way musical data are recorded on a cassette tape in a home music system.

"Because the surface of the disk is hard and very flat," Connoly went on, "it is possible to position or 'float' the `head' that reads and writes data very close to the surface of the disk. This makes it possible to record data in such a way that the circular **tracks** in which data are stored can be positioned very close to one another. So a hard disk can pack in many more tracks than can a floppy disk. In addition a hard disk system packs the data within each track closer together. These factors explain why hard disks have such large data storage capacity. And the fact that these disks rotate much faster than floppy disks explains why it is possible to get to data faster -- hence faster access times."

O'Brien then asked if this was the reason why it took so long for his current sytem to retrieve data.

"Not entirely," was Connoly's reply. "Your system has organized and stored your data **sequentially**. This means that your accounts receivable records, for example, are stored in the same order they are entered. And they can only be retrieved sequentially in this order. Let's suppose you wanted to retrieve the record for Silver Brothers, one of your customers. If their record was stored at the end of your file, then to access the record your software would issue instructions to start at the beginning of the file and proceed forward until the Silver Brothers record was found. Since it is at the end of the file, this retrieval process could take many seconds. You can also see why it takes longer and longer to retrieve records as your file grows with new records.

"The new system will work differently," he went on. "Data will be organized **randomly** on the hard disk. What this means is that they are scattered throughout the disk in what may seem to be a random location. But it is this form of organization that supports **direct access**, in which records can be accessed nearly instantly and in any order."

O'Brien asked, "If the data are stored randomly throughout the disk, how does the system know were to find data when a request is made?"

"There are different ways. Our system builds an index, much like the card catalog index in a library, which helps you locate a book in the stacks. The computer index stores the record key -- a primary identifier of a record such as the shipper's ID number -- and the physical address or location where the data are stored on the disk. Then when a record needs to be accessed, the index is automatically searched and the address at which the record is stored is read. Once the address is known the system then directs the read/write head to proceed to the appropriate location on the disk."

BACKUP PROCEDURES

"All of this sounds impressive," said O'Brien. "But is all of this 'high tech' reliable? I heard about a company that lost its accounts receivable data when its disk 'crashed.' It was a costly error from which they never recovered."

"The system will be as safe as the procedures you use to protect your data," Connoly said. " You'll have to decide on backup procedures. There are three basic choices. First, you can buy a second hard disk and duplicate all entries. The likelihood that both will crash is very small. But this will be an expensive solution. As another alternative, you can periodically copy your hard disk to floppy disks using the floppy drive on the minicomputer. But this will take an operator a long time to complete. It could take ten or more floppies to store the data, and it will take a few minutes to transfer the data to each floppy. Another approach is to use a `streaming' tape drive. New sytems use a four-inch-square tape cartridge with a capacity of about 200 MB. The tape can be inserted into a tape drive and the disk backed up without the need for operator intervention. Some drives even back up the disk at regular intervals automatically.

QUESTIONS

1. What type of computer and off-line storage system is Coastal using now?
2. What disadvantages does O'Brien find with the current system?

3. The time it takes clerks to retrieve a record from Coastal's current accounts receivable system can be quite long. Why?
4. Why is the current system inconvenient?
5. In general, describe the new system. Use such terms as minicomputer, multiuser, multiaccess, and hard disk.
6. Describe a hard disk. How does its capacity compare with that of a floppy disk? How do the access times compare?
7. With a floppy disk system a new disk must be inserted into the disk drive whenever a new application is run. Is this true of a hard drive system also?
8. Explain why hard disks have larger capacities and faster access times than do floppy disks.
9. What is meant by sequential organization on disk?
10. The current system organizes and accesses data sequentially. Why is this a problem in this application?
11. What is direct or random organization? What advantage does it have over sequential organization in the application described in the case?
12. How would data be located in the randomly organized disk file associated with the new system?
13. "Hard disks are very reliable and thereby make it unnecessary for data to be backed up on other storage media." Do you agree with this statement? Why or why not?
14. Which of the three alternatives described in the case would you use to back up data? Why?

QUIK INC.

Quik Inc., an overnight package delivery service with customers in all 50 states, was losing ground to its competitors. The reason: fierce competition. If a competitor introduced a better or less expensive service, the customer switched. In this business there was little "brand loyalty."

A NEW COMPUTER SYSTEM

At the company's annual strategic planning meeting, held this year in Palm Beach, Florida, the VP of marketing, Sumner Rand, proposed an on-line customer system in which customers, using their own computers, would enter pickup and delivery requests directly into Quik's computer system. If customers needed to have a package picked up, for example, they would access Quik's computer through the telephone network and enter the delivery information into their own terminals. The data would instantly update Quik's database and a request for pickup would be transmitted instantly to a driver close to the customer's location. In addition to entering pickup orders, customers could trace the whereabouts of any package once it had been picked up. They could find out were it was located or if it had aready been delivered.

"If we give our customers access to our computer system," said Sumner Rand, "we've got a competitive advantage that will be hard to beat!"

Although the proposal sounded good to many at the meeting, it was the director of MIS, Steve Woods, that seemed most concerned about its potential.

IS IT TOO COMPLEX?

Woods began his response to this proposal with an overview of the current system and its problems. "Our system basically supports the accounting, customer billing, payroll, accounts receivable, and accounts payable functions. To also record, store, and track the whereabouts of packages with this system would be impossible. It's already overloaded. We would definitely need a new computer system. And we would need an army of data collection terminals positioned at points where the packages first enter our transportation system, and at points where the packages are transferred to other modes of transportation.

"Besides all that," Woods went on, "we would need software to manage the database of customer data, and communication software that would permit our customers to access the systemm. You're talking about a very complex system. I'm not so sure it's feasible."

During this meeting they discussed the possible benefits, costs, and disadvantages of such a system. But no consensus was reached to continue or abandon the idea. Soon the conversation turned to other issues.

The group returned from Florida to find revenues short of targets once again. Then, about two weeks later, the president, Tammy Brentwood, asked Woods to look into the customer tracking system more carefully.

DATA REQUIREMENTS

Woods enlisted two of his top people and began a preliminary study. One of these people, Alex Foley, was assigned the job of looking into the data storage requirements of such a system.

Within a few days Foley reached several conclusions. It would be essential for the new system to be on-line. This meant that the system had to be capable of processing a request to store or retrieve data instantaneously.The system needed hard disk storage. A hard disk is built on a rigid aluminum platter and utilizes **Winchester technology** in which the disk is permanently sealed to protect it from environmental contamination. The disk rotates at speeds of 3600 revolutions per minute and because it is built to such fine tolerances, data can be packed densely around its concentric rings or tracks. A read/write head, like the arm of a turntable in a home stereo system, is used to read and write data to the tracks. It is moved to a given track and reads or writes data as the appropriate location on the track passes under the head.

The time between requesting data and receiving the response on the screen, **access time**, is very short on the type of disk that Woods is considering -- betwen 15 and 30 milliseconds (a **millisecond** is 1/1000 of a second).

DATA ORGANIZATION AND ACCESS

Data can be organized on the disk in one of two ways, sequential and random. This application would call for random organization. In **random organization** the data are scattered throughout the disk in what might seem to be a random order. The advantage is that this organization supports **direct access**, in which records can be accessed instantly. Customers would therefore be able to determine the location and status of their packages within a few seconds at most.

Since the data are scattered randomly throughout the disk there must be a mechanism to find where the data are stored. An **index** will serve this purpose. It will contain the customer ID and the location of the customer's record. Whenever access to the record is needed, the customer will enter its ID, the system will automatically refer to an index -- which is actually a separate file -- and after reading the physical location from the index, will instruct the read/write head to proceed to the appropriate track and read the appropriate record as it passes below the head.

Woods had his staff take a preliminary look into other aspects of the proposed system, including the computer that would be needed, database management software for managing the database of customer data (the software would be responsible for developing and using the index described earlier), remote terminals for data collection, and communication requirements to tie together customers and the central computer.

SECURITY CONCERNS

During its final meeting the group was particularly concerned about opening up a database to customers. Sally Friedman thought that this would mean Quik Inc. would have little control over the accuracy of the data and over who was entitled to use it. "Would it be possible for one of our customer's competitors to dial up our computer, gain access to the database and then learn who our customers were selling to? While we gained a competitive advantage they could lose theirs," she questioned. Everyone agreed that protecting the data would be an important issue in the design of the system.

FEASIBLITY REPORT

Once this preliminary study was finished they prepared a feasibility report. It presented the objectives of the system, user requirements, a preliminary description of the hardware and software that would be needed, and the storage requirements that Foley had studied. The report concluded by stating that this would be a major project, larger than any MIS project that Quik had undertaken to date, and its cost could be as high $20 million, with up to three years required for completion.

QUESTIONS

1. Why is Quik considering this new system?
2. Describe the system.
3. How is Quik's present computer system used? Can it be expanded to include this new application?
4. How will Quik benefit from this system? Will lower costs or increased revenues result? Explain.
5. Describe the disk that will be used for data storage. What is Winchester technology? What is access time? How is access time measured?
6. Do you think a microcomputer with two floppy disk drives could be used for this application? Why or why not?
7. Why is access time important to the end-user?
8. What is random organization?
9. How are records found in the type of system which Woods is considering?
10. While the "mean time between failures," a measure of the reliability of hard disks, is very high, disks do "crash" and the data are lost. What measures can be taken to protect the data in this application?
11. Friedman feels that a system open to customers could be abused. Do you agree? What safegaurds could be taken to prevent this?
12. "If you let customers enter their own pickup and delivery data they could enter incorrect data and the entire system would fall apart. It is much better to use a central facility in which professional sales reps answer the phone and enter the information into a terminal." Do you agree or disagree with this statement? Why?

S E C T I O N 5

FILE MANAGERS

One of the best-kept secrets in end-user computing is that you don't *have* to use complicated database management systems in order to handle many applications. A **file manager** can often do the job instead. File managers are a lot easier to use, cost less, and present fewer headaches. They are also less powerful, particularly in being able to deal with only one file at a time.

As the concepts surrounding files and databases are confusing, this section and the next attempt to clarify them. In the cases presented in this section two specific applications of file managers are described. The first case, Todd Publishing, shows how a salesperson can improve record keeping concerning clients, thereby avoiding missed opportunities. The second case, Hayden Construction, demonstrates that the three by five index cards many people still use probably should be retired. In both instances the file managers at the heart of the applications can be understood and applied by their busy users with only a small investment of time.

TODD PUBLISHING

Todd Publishing, established in 1952, is a textbook publisher with some 350 titles in such areas as philosophy, English, engineering, and nursing. Todd is primarily a basic book publisher, one that focuses on the entry level courses in two-year and four-year schools. They publish few texts for upper division courses.

COLLEGE TRAVELERS

When Janice Hood graduated from college three years ago she took a job with Todd. One of 150 "college travelers," who call on instructors, Todd introduces appropriate books to them and works with them during the book adoption process. To be effective in her job, Hood must not only understand the books she sells, she must also be familiar with competitive books from other publishers.

Hood covers 15 schools in a three-state region. Only a few are large schools with enrollments over 10,000 students; the rest are smaller schools with average enrollments of 2000 students. Although taken together the schools that Hood visits have over 9000 faculty members, the titles that Todd publishes are appropriate for about 4000 of the faculty members.

During the first two years Hood was busy familiarizing herself with the titles in Todd's line and with the faculty members in those departments where these titles would be appropriate candidates for adoption.

INDEX CARDS

As she reflected about her first two years, Hood felt that one aspect of her job that needed improving was the way she organized the information she used to organize her campus visits. Until now she had used file cards. Although she did not find it difficult to write notes on the cards and file them in her file boxes, it was very difficult to search these files on anything but a superficial basis. For example, last October Todd published a title in psychology that had been reviewed very well during the development of the text. Everyone at Todd felt they had a winner. The marketing manager for social sciences sent a memo to all travelers suggesting that they push for January adoptions, even though the selection process for the second semester had alrady occurred at some schools or was well underway. Hood went to her file box to locate the names of professors who taught this couse.

But the search was a lengthy one. It took several hours, and she probably missed a few.

She wondered if there was an easier way.

A SIMPLE COMPUTER FILING SYSTEM

There was. At the national sales conference in St. Louis, Hood found her answer. A colleague, Herb Shapiro, had developed a simple computer filing system, like the one she needed. Shapiro explained that he purchased a category of file management software that is classified as a **file manager**. This category -- while it can only accommodate a single file at a time -- is perfectly adequate for the kinds of data that many people need to store and retrieve.

"This system is relatively easy to use," Shapiro said. "I just tell it what I want, and the software determines the details necessary to execute the request and then oversees the process of getting the job done. There is no need for me to write programs or to understand any of the details of the data storage and retrieval process. All I have to know is the general proceedures for managing data."

"Could you describe them to me?" asked Hood.

"Every data management system, not just file managers, must be able to do several things," Shapiro said. "First, the system must lead the user through the process of creating the file. In this process the user will specify the name of the file and the fields of data in it. Usually no data are entered at this point -- just the structure of the file is specified.

"Here's the file system I created," Shapiro continued. He showed Hood a sheet of paper with the names of the fields of data on it (Figure 1).

"Second, the software must also be able to accept data entered by the user," Shapiro continued. "Usually a screen appears on the terminal which lists the names of the data fields that you entered, and the user then enters the specific data for one record at a time.

"Third, the system must be to retrieve data. To do this the user enters a record key -- the identifier of a record such as a person's social security number or, in this application, a professor's name -- and the software automatically locates the record and displays the result on the screen. So in our applications, if we wanted to see the data stored on Professor Thomas, we would type in her name, and then the record -- with all of the fields of data specified when the file was created -- would be displayed on the screen.

"Fourth, the software must be capable of producing reports," Shapiro went on. "And here is where it is most helpful to us. Suppose you needed a report that listed all professors who teach introductory psychology. First, you would design the layout of the report, then you would specify the particular course -- in this case psychology -- for which you need a printout, and then the report would be printed.

PROFESSOR'S NAME:
SCHOOL:
STREET ADDRESS:
CITY:
STATE:
ZIP CODE:
TELEPHONE NUMBER:
OFFICE ROOM NUMBER:
OFFICE HOURS:
DEPARTMENT:
COURSE TAUGHT 1:
COURSE TAUGHT 2:
COURSE TAUGHT 3:
COURSE TAUGHT 4:
COURSE TAUGHT 5:

Figure 1.   The structure of the "college traveler" file.

using the data contained in the file. Later, you might want to use this same report format but listing all profesors who teach introductory economics. With the report writer in my file manager, this would be an easy job.

"Fifth, the software, in addition to accepting new data as I just described, must also be capable of accommodating updates. So if a professor teaches a new course, then his or her record can be updated to include this new data item.

"Although there are other functions a file manager can perform," Shapiro continued, "these are the major ones and should give you an idea of what file managers do. If you want, I could send you a copy of some of my reports. If you like them, I could help you set up a system."

"Herb, can we go back to your file structure for a minute?" Hood asked.

"Sure, what would you like to know?"

"It seems to me that in addition to the courses that a professor taught I would like to know the books -- both ours and our competitors -- used for those courses. And don't you think it would be useful to also include a separate field that lists the books a professor uses in each of the courses which are taught? If I save this kind of information, then the file would be even more useful to me. I could ask for a list of all those professors who use Stevenson's chemistry book, say, or I could print a list of all professors in my region who use our new calculus book."

QUESTIONS

1. How does Hood use her manual filing system?
2. Why has Hood's file system proven unsatisfactory?
3. Why might it be useful for Hood to computerize her file system?
4. What is a file manager?
5. Describe the functions performed by a file manager.
6. With a file manager, what is an update? How does it differ from the process of entering data for the first time?
7. How much detail about the data storage and retrieval process must a file manager user understand and be prepared to use?
8. What is a report?
9. How is a report prepared with a file manager?
10. Expand the file structure used by Shapiro to include the fields suggested by Hood. How can the new data be used?
11. Why do you think the street address, city, state, and zip code are stored in separate fields? In the interest of saving storage space, should they be combined in a single "address field?"

HAYDEN CONSTRUCTION

Hayden Construction is a general contractor specializing in the construction of commercial buildings. While they maintain a workforce of over 150 carpenters, masons, electricians, and plumbers, they frequently need to call on independent subcontractors to supplement their workforce.

RETRIEVING DATA IS A PROBLEM

Until a year ago the office maintained a 3- by 5- card index file to help locate these firms. The file contained the information shown in Figure 1.

NAME:
STREET ADDRESS:
TOWN:
STATE:
ZIP CODE:
TELEPHONE NUMBER:
TRADE:
CONTACT PERSON:
WORKFORCE SIZE:
HOURLY RATE PER WORKER:

Figure 1. Hayden independent subcontractor file.

The file system grew to about 800 entries, and because it became so large, searching for information was very inefficient. On one occasion, for example, the company was behind on a job in a small town located about 100 miles away. They needed electricians and plumbers. It took several hours for a secretary to search the file for plumbers and electricians whose addresses were close to the construction site.

The office manager, Chris O'Shea, used spreadsheet and word processing software regularly. O'Shea asked an accountant at the public accounting firm that

```
MAIN MENU

1 Design file    4 Search/Update
2 Add            5 Print
3 Copy           6 Remove

Selection:   1
File Name:   TRADE
```

```
DESIGN FILE MENU

1 Create file
2 Change design

Selection:   1
```

```
NAME:
STREET ADDRESS:
TOWN:
STATE:
ZIP CODE:
TELEPHONE NUMBER:
TRADE:
CONTACT PERSON:
WORKFORCE SIZE:
HOURLY RATE:
```

Figure 2.   Building the file manager system.

did Hayden's accounting if spreadsheet software could be used to maintain the 3-by-5 card file on a computer. The accountant suggested that file manager software would be a better choice. File manager software would store the data for each tradesperson, would update the file when changes were necessary, and would prepare reports like the ones needed to identify appropriate tradespeople in a hurry.

O'Shea ordered PFS, a popular file manager program, and began the job of designing a system. He began using it six months ago.

HOW THE FILE MANAGER SYSTEM WORKS

The first step in using this system is to create the file.

O'Shea placed the software disk in one drive of the microcomputer and a blank disk that would store the file of data in the other drive. The first screen that appeared on the micro (Figure 2) presented a **menu**, or selection of choices, and O'Shea chose the "design file" option. He entered the number 1 and followed this with a carriage return. Then he entered the file name, "Trade."

In response the micro displayed a new menu screen. O'Shea chose the "create file" option. The screen that followed was blank, and he began entering the name of each field in his file. No data are actually entered at this time, only the field names. These names will establish the structure of the file into which the data will then be entered.

The file is then built by entering the data from the 3-by-5 index cards. In this step the user returns to the main menu and selects "Add." Next, the name of the file is entered, and then a screen appears that displays the field names that were entered when the file was originally created. The cursor is then positioned at the first field, and the data are entered. When a return is pressed, the cursor will move to the next field. The process is repeated until all the data for the record have been entered. After the data for the last field have been entered, the record is stored, and another screen, showing the field names, appears on the main screen ready for entry of the data for the next record.

To retrieve data from a file once it has been created, the user starts again at the main menu, selects the "search" option, and enters the name of the file. A screen will appear that includes the names of the fields. The user then enters the criterion by which the file should be searched. For example, suppose it is necessary to retrieve the telephone number for Sorrell Plumbing. The user would enter "Sorrell Plumbing" in the name field followed by a return. The computer would then display the data contained in the record for Sorrell Plumbing.

Records can also be retrieved by using relational operators. A **relational operator** is an algebraic sign, such as < (less than), <= (less than or equal to), = (equal to), and > (greater than). Suppose a listing was needed of all plumbers with a crew of more than 30 workers. The database could be searched by entering "> 30" into the "workforce" field.

THE SYSTEM PROVES ITSELF

The file manager system was a big improvement over the manual methods used before. With the file manager, when additional workers are needed for a job, the computer provides a list in a few minutes. And the big difference is that Hayden is calling subcontractors that they never called before, and often calling those whose hourly rates are lower than ones they used before.

CHANGES

Three weeks ago O'Shea left the company. The person hired to replace him, Joyce Woo, had used file manager software before. Although she liked the system that was in place at Hayden, she decided it could be better. First, she concluded that they needed some measure of the "on-time" performance of these subcontractors. She decided on a scheme like that shown in Figure 3.

LATE	ON-TIME RATING
0 WEEKS	A
1-2 WEEKS	B
2-4 WEEKS	C
> 4 WEEKS	D

Figure 3. On-time measure for subcontractors

In addition to the lateness factor, she also decided that a quality factor would be helpful in selecting subcontractors (Figure 4).

QUALITY	QUALITY RATING
EXCELLENT	A
GOOD	B
AVERAGE	C
POOR	D

Figure 4. Quality factor measure for subcontractors

In her third week at Hayden, Woo began to make the changes in the system. To update the file to include these ratings she talked with several of the people in the firm, including the foremen, and established on-time and quality ratings for most of the subcontractors. She then loaded the file manager software, selected the "design file" option, and then selected "change design" and entered the new fields. Next, she entered these two fields of data for each record through the "add" option in the main menu.

QUESTIONS

1. Describe the manual system originally used. Why was it replaced?
2. What is a file manager system?
3. What is a data disk?
4. Describe how a file is created.
5. What steps are followed to enter the data when a file is first created?
6. Suppose a new subcontractor calls Hayden and is interested in picking up work. What data would be collected, and how would it be entered? Start from the main menu. Which option would be selected?
7. Work is behind on a project in the Riversview area. How would you locate subcontractors? Describe the process step by step.
8. Describe the steps necessary to list all subcontractors whose hourly rate is less than or equal to $25 per hour per worker.
9. What changes did Woo make to the system?
10. Do you think these changes will help in selecting subcontractors? Explain.
11. Static data, like an address, are those data in a file that change infrequently if at all. Dynamic data change frequently. How would you classify the performance rating data -- static or dynamic?
12. Every data management system, including file mangers and database management systems, must have the capability to create, add data to, update, and retrieve data from the file or database. Expain how the file manager software illustrated in this case meets these needs.

DATABASE
MANAGEMENT SYSTEMS

The file managers described in the last section are appropriate for many applications, but not for those involving extensive input and output operations, the need for more than one file, or use by a number of different programs. A **database management system (DBMS)** offers a more powerful alternative, one that is widely used today. Applications range from end-users working with stand-alone microcomputers to mammoth databases maintained and used by federal government agencies and major corporations.

The three cases presented here attempt to clarify the main characteristics of database management systems and their use. At Magna Machine, in the first case, a DBMS makes it possible to link together data contained in an employee background file and a job file. Great Plains Insurance, in the second case, faces the necessity of switching to a DBMS for the sake of sanity and efficiency in handling its millions of records on customer policies. In the third case, the Coral Bay Hotel sees use of a DBMS as a means of better serving its guests and improving its bottom line.

MAGNA MACHINE

Charlie Zeckel was involved in the design of an employee history file for his division. Zeckel, the personnel manager, had obtained a copy of a file manager software package, but was having trouble fitting the data into the appropriate format.

Magna Machine was a division of Southern Bay Electric, a manufacturer of electrical equipment and household appliances. Magna produces small electric engines used primarily in industrial control applications, and employs 1500 full-time hourly workers and 200 salaried employees.

Zeckel walked over to Doug Sanders in the MIS department and asked if they could spend a few minutes together. Zeckel explained his problem to Sanders. "We need to put our employee job history on computer. First we need to store data about the employee -- name, employee ID, address, social security number, home telephone, office telephone, date of birth, date of hire, year of school completed, degree, and previous employer. Then we need to keep records for each job held at Magna. These records should include a description of the position, the job level classification, the hourly rate or salary, the supervisor or manager's name, the date the postion was started, and the date the position was terminated.

"As you know," Zeckel went on, "employees change jobs or job classifications regularly. Since we want to keep the old data as well as add the new job status, I designed a system where each time a change takes place we establish a new record in the file." At this point Zeckel produced a sketch of the file (Figure 1).

"But I'm not really happy with this approach," Zeckel said, "because there could be 20 to 30 records for each employee, and I think it would be hard to keep them straight."

EMPLOYEE NAME:
EMPLOYEE ID:
ADDRESS:
SOCIAL SECURITY NUMBER:
HOME TELEPHONE:
OFFICE TELEPHONE:
DATE OF BIRTH:
YEAR OF HIRE:
LAST YEAR OF SCHOOL COMPLETED:
DEGREE EARNED:

PREVIOUS EMPLOYER:
POSITION DESCRIPTION:
JOB CLASSIFICATION:
PAY RATE:
SUPERVISOR:
START DATE:
END DATE:

Figure 1. Employee file at Magna.

TOO MANY FILES

Sanders pointed out that the reason Zeckel was having a problem was that he was looking at the data structure in the wrong way, and that he was using the wrong type of data management software. "What you need," Sanders said, "is not a file manager but a database management system. We call that a DBMS. The file manager you are using can only handle one file at a time, and the data you want to store should be divided into two files. To handle more than one file you have to have a DBMS."

Sanders began by drawing a diagram of the logical relationship between the data in these files (Figure 2). "This diagram is called a **schema**," he said. "It is a logical view of all the data in a database. We call it a **logical view** because it describes the way that people look at the data. The data may actually be stored in a very different way in the computer, but we don't have to worry about that. The job of the software is to link our logical view with the way that data are stored, or the **physical view**.

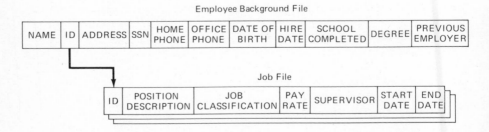

Figure 2. The schema shows how records in one file are linked to records in another

"As you can see from my sketch we will have two files," Sanders went on. "The first we can call the 'employee background file' and the second the 'job file.' The employee background file will include the employee's name, employee ID, address, social security number, home telephone, office telephone, date of birth, date of hire, last year of school completed, degree earned, and previous employer.

"Now we come to the second file," Sanders continued. "In this file a separate record will be established every time a job classification or raise is granted to an employee. This file will include the employee's ID, position description, job classification, pay rate, supervisor, start date, and end date. To illustrate this with an example, suppose John Smith has recived three raises and two job reclassifications; then there would be one employee background record and five job history records.

"And now we come to an important characteristic of a DBMS. The job of the software is to link the record in the employee background file to the appropriate number of records in the job history file. This link is established through the record's primary key. The primary key is the unique identifier of a record. It must appear in the record contained in the employee background file and also in every record contained in the job history file. In your case the primary key would be the employee ID. You can see (Figure 2) how I included this ID not only in the employee background file but in the job history file. Notice also that I drew an arrow between these fields to make it clear how they are related or linked. It's worth emphasizing that the reason this is an important characteristic of a DBMS is because it is through this mechanism that we can link two or more files together when we need to retrieve information from the system."

MINIMIZING REDUNDANT DATA

"And because we can link the employee background file with the job history file," Sanders went on, "we need only store the employee background information once. In the file manager system you tried to develop, you needed to store the employee background data on every new job history record. So in the case of Mr. Smith you would have entered these data five different times. Not only would this have resulted in redundant data in the database -- and remember, data storage space is limited and costly -- but it is more than likely that the data in many of those records could have been wrong."

"How would they be wrong?" Zeckel asked.

"Well, let me give an example," Sanders replied. "If Smith's telephone number changed and if one of your staff looked up an older job classification record to get his number, they would have retrieved the wrong one. With my DBMS system, you only store one telephone number. Storing something once is a lot less confusing and usually much more accurate.

"Charlie," Sanders concluded, "why don't you design your system on a DBMS? In the long run that would be the right way to go."

QUESTIONS

1. Describe the file manager system that Zeckel was in the process of designing.
2. How many files of data were contained in the file manager system?
3. Suppose an employee had been with the company for ten years and had received eight raises and four job reclassifications. How many records, using a file manager system, would be stored in the computer system?
4. What is a DBMS?
5. What is a schema?
6. Explain the schema shown in Figure 10.
7. Why are two files used in Figure 10?
8. How does a DBMS minimize redundant data? Does it completely eliminate redundant data?
9. Explain why data in a DBMS might be more accurate than data stored in a file manager system.
10. How are data from two files in a DBMS linked together when it is necessary to retrieve information?
11. Would you agree with Sanders that a DBMS should be used? Why.

GREAT PLAINS MUTUAL LIFE

The MIS department at the Great Plains Mutual Life Insurance Company is becoming bogged down with work. Because they are responsible for maintaining a growing number of computer applications, the MIS department has less and less time available for developing new applications or responding to requests from the professional staff to supply them with special reports.

Great Plains has nearly two million customers, many of whom have more than one policy in force. Computer information systems play a significant role in serving these customers and maintaining records on their policies.

To support these record keeping needs, Great Plains uses an IBM mainframe. According to Jerry Work, director of MIS, the record keeping applications are supported by 28 databases. These databases are made up of some 270 files that occupy 50 IBM disk drives. The largest file contains more than four million records and is stored on three IBM model 3380 drives.

CONVENTIONAL FILE PROCESSING

The 28 databases used to store data are not managed by a database management system. This approach -- common at one time -- is known as **conventional file processing**. Conventional file processing has several drawbacks when it is compared to the use of a DBMS to manage data. Applications can be more difficult to develop and those who are not computer professionals may find it impossible to access the database.

A Database Management System, or DBMS, is a collection of programs that manages and controls a database, providing the means through which data items can be stored, retrieved, and changed.

Work is proposing that Great Plains convert to a DBMS. A conversion such as this will represent a project of major proportions, and could take several years to complete. However, he explained to a group of Great Plains managers, "we can't possibly achieve our productivity goals with our conventional system. It is just costing us too much time and effort to build new applications and, more important, to maintain the ones we have. We should move to a DBMS."

WHAT A DBMS HAS TO OFFER

"A DBMS should provide Great Plains with several advantages," Work explained. "First, the DBMS will perfom most of the data management tasks itself. With our conventional file processing system we have to write all of the detailed instructions necessary to access and retrieve data. With a DBMS we just have to tell the system what we want, and the DBMS software figures out the details of how to do it. What this means is that we write less code. An instruction using a conventional system might take several hundred lines of COBOL code, while it may take only a few lines of instructions in the DBMS language. Usually these sytems increase productivity by five to twenty-five times.

"Another advantage," Work went on, "is that a DBMS separates the database from the application programs. The present sytem does not. This means that if a change is made in the database, all the programs that use the data must also be changed. Recently a field size in one of our databases was increased from 25 to 35 characters. All of the programs which read the file in which this field was stored had to be revised to read this larger field. Eight people had to assigned to this to meet the target date. With a DBMS this would not have been necessary. The DBMS would have separated the database from the applications, so that a change in a field size would not have required this change to each program. The result -- much less work for us.

"Our system also includes a lot of redundant data. Many of our policyholders have more than one policy. But since our 28 databases are totally separate, certain data about each policyholder are stored in several files. If a policyholder has four policies, then we will store his or her name and other personal data in four different files. Not only does this waste space, but it opens us up for errors. It's not uncommon, for example, for one of these customers to send us a change of address and for us to update some, but not all, of the policies held in this person's name. The result is that some correspondence goes to the old address. But with a DBMS, the files are structured in such a way that links can be made between the files. As a result we need to store such data as names and addresses in only one file. Connections can then be made between the data in this one file and other files that store the data concerning each of the policies the customer holds. Because we can establish these linkages or **relationships**, redundancy is minimized."

Karen Logan, vice-president of finance, asked how this new system could benefit the professional business staff.

Work explained that with the DBMS he had in mind it would be easier for the MIS staff to develop management reports. "With the present system we have to write lengthy COBOL programs every time a new report is developed. But with the DBMS, development be simplified; we only have to tell the software what we want, and it will determine the detailed steps necessary to produce the report. Some users claim that the increase in productivity for developing reports is about

25 times. As you can see, we have the time to be more responsive to the business staff's needs.

"Karen, there is another advantage that will affect you directly," continued Work. "The DBMS comes with a **query language**. This a language interface that makes it relatively simple for a non-MIS professional like those on our business staff to retrieve information. I would say that with about one day of training and a few days of experience, anyone on the staff would be able to make simple requests and retrieve data from the system. I would think that the young people would be especially eager to try this, and I am sure that this could help reduce the intolerable backlog of requests that users have sent us."

QUESTIONS

1. What is conventional file processing?
2. Describe the disadvantages of conventional file processing.
3. At the present time how does the MIS department spend most of its time? How responsive are they to the business professionals on the Great Plains staff?
4. What is data redundancy? How does a DBMS solve this problem?
5. What is a DBMS?
6. What is the consequence of separating the data in the database from the application programs? Is this possible with conventional file processing?
7. Does a DBMS improve the productivity of the programming staff? Explain.
8. How does a DBMS help business professionals?
9. Can a DBMS help reduce the backlog of requests in an MIS department? If so, how?
10. Summarize the reasons why Great Plains should convert to a DBMS. Include both the benefits and costs in your answer.

CORAL BAY HOTEL

The Coral Bay Hotel, located on the east end of St. John, American Virgin Islands, is a 135-room, full-service hotel. It includes a restaurant, a coffee shop, two bars, and a gift shop. Sales last year were over $4 million.

The hotel was recently sold to Phil Curran, who had worked for a Fortune 500 company for over 20 years. In Curran's words, he bought the place because he needed a change.

Hotel services with the exception of room charges are provided on a cash-only basis. Customers who patronize the restuarants, snack bar, or lounges must pay by cash or credit card when a purchase is made. And hotel guests must also pay at the time they rent sailboats, windsurfing boards, or snorkel gear.

NEW METHODS

When Curran arrived from Chicago not only did he bring new ideas, but he also brought an IBM PS/20 model 60, together with word processing, spreadsheet, and database management software. He was confident that if he developed a customer billing system and eliminated the requirement for hotel guests to pay when served, expenditure per guest would increase by at least ten percent. In addition, he felt that the system would provide a valuable service to his guests who would prefer not to pay several times each day, but rather once at the end of their stay.

The system Curran would design would include the data shown in Figure 1. In

NAME:
ADDRESS:
TELEPHONE NUMBER:
METHOD OF PAYMENT; CASH, CREDIT CARD, CHECK:
CREDIT CARD NUMBER:
NUMBER OF GUESTS:
ROOM NUMBER:
ROOM RATE:
DATE IN:
DATE OUT:

Figure 1. Guest data for the new Coral Bay Hotel system.

addition, the data shown in Figure 2 would have to be stored every time a guest made a purchase.

ROOM NUMBER:

DATE:

TYPE OF SERVICE; FOOD, DRINK, RENTAL:

CHARGE:

TAX:

Figure 2. Charge data for the new Coral Bay Hotel system.

SCHEMA FOR THE NEW SYSTEM

Curran would develop the application using his database management system. To begin, he had to separate the data into two files, one containing the data shown in Figure 1 and the other containing the data shown in Figure 2. A more visual way to describe the logic behind this separation into two files can be shown in a schema. A **schema** is a logical view of all of the data in a database. It is called a **logical view** because it represents the way users see the data rather than the way in which the data are physically stored on the disk

Users need only to design a system from a logical point of view. It is the responsibility of the database managment software to link the logical view to the way in which data storage will actually take place, called the **physical view**.

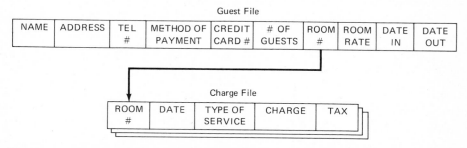

Figure 3. The schema for the new system shows the fields in each of the two files and how these files are related.

The schema for this application is shown in Figure 3. The first file is called the guest file, and the second is called the charge file. When a guest arrives, a new record in the guest file would be established by the system. The name, address, credit card number, and other data would be entered into this record. The second file contains a separate record for each new charge. So if a guest incurred 32 charges in a week, there would be one guest record and 32 charge records.

KEN WESTON
32 JUNKINS COURT
HUNTINGTON CT 06484

ARRIVAL DATE   2/12   DEPARTURE DATE 2/14

NUMBER OF GUESTS   3
ROOM RATE/DAY $225

2/12	ROOM	225.00
	ROOM TAX	16.87
	DINNER	84.50
	DRINKS	32.75
2/13	ROOM	225.00
	ROOM TAX	16.87
	BREAKFAST	21.00
	LUNCH	12.75
	DRINKS	3.50
	DINNER	55.00
2/14	BREAKFAST	10.75
	TOTAL	703.99

Figure 4. A bill like the one shown above retrieves data from two related files in the database.

NAME	ADDRESS	TEL #	METHOD OF PAYMENT	CREDIT CARD #	# OF GUESTS	ROOM #	ROOM RATE	DATE IN	DATE OUT
KEN WESTON	32 JUNKINS COURT HUNTINGTON CT 06484	312-643-2771	CC	27152114	3	142	225	2/12	2/14
NANCY WILCOX	1742 MAIN ST LOS ANGELES CA 95112	213-411-1789	CHECK	————	1	161	175	2/12	2/15

ROOM #	DATE	TYPE OF SERVICE	CHARGE	TAX
142	2/12	ROOM	225.00	16.87
161	2/12	ROOM	175.00	13.12
142	2/12	DINNER	84.50	
141	2/12	DRINKS	25.00	
142	2/12	DRINKS	32.75	
161	2/12	DINNER	21.50	
142	2/13	ROOM	225	16.87

Figure 5. The data in a relational database can be expressed as a set of tables. To produce a bill like the one shown in Figure 4, the relational database software would link these tables through the room number.

A RELATIONAL DBMS

The categorty of database management system Curran used is called a **relational DBMS**. One of the reasons it is called "relational" is because it has the ability to relate records in one file with records in another. This feature is needed, for example, to relate a guest's record in the guest file with his or her charges in the billing file. Once related, reports can be produced which draw data from both files. Suppose the front desk needed to print a bill for Ken Weston like the one shown in Figure 4. Some of the data would come from the guest file and some from the charge file.

In order to relate the data in one file with specific data in another file, it is necessary to link them in a unique way. As you can see from the arrow in Figure 3, Curran will link them with the room number. The room number, then, must appear as a field in both files.

Here is how the linkage worked in the example just described. When a bill was requested for Weston, the system searched the second file for all entries with Weston's room number. The bill, actually a "report," then included data from Weston's record in the guest file and only charges made to his room number.

Although it is useful to use the concept of a schema to understand the logical structure of the data in a database, a logical view of a relational database is often expressed as a set of tables, in which the data for each file are stored in a separate table. An example of the data that might be in the two databases is shown in Figure 5.

QUESTIONS

1. Describe the purpose of the system Curran will design.
2. What fields of data will be stored by the system?
3. Why is a database management system necessary in this application?
4. What is a schema?
5. Does a schema represent a logical or physical view of the data? Explain.
6. Describe the schema in this application.
7. Suppose a guest stays at the hotel for five days and incurs five charges for room costs (including room tax), twelve food charges, and three rental charges. How many records would be established?
8. What are relationships in a database?
9. Explain how relationships are used to produce a report.
10. Why can't Curran include all of the necessary data for each guest in one record, and thereby reduce the complexity of the system by putting everything in one file?

SECTION 7

SYSTEMS ANALYSIS AND DESIGN

Many business professionals today inevitably become involved in the process of systems analysis and design. This does not mean that they need to be expert programmers, systems analysts, or engineers, but that a general grasp of the system analysis and design process will profitably supplement their all-important user's point of view.

The cases in this section show four diverse, modern organizations that have recognized a problem or opportunity.

In each case the means of solving the problem, or seizing the opportunity, is a new or revised computer information system. These cases involve conflicting points of view and few immediately clear answers, as is typical in the early stages of systems analysis and design, when an organization faces a process that may cost millions of dollars and take years to complete.

VISTA HOSPITAL

Vista Hospital, a 460-bed hospital located in a major city on the West Coast, began using computers over 15 years ago. The hospital first started with patient billing and accounts receivable systems, which bill patients for the services provided and keep track of the amounts owed and payments received from patients and insurance companies. In the early 1980s Vista added registration to the system. When a person enters the hospital, patient data such as name, address, and insurance carrier are entered into this module. The system stores registration data on-line so that the data can be retrieved and billing data added during that hospital stay. The patient financial record is permanently stored on hard disk and can also be retrieved if the patient is admitted again at a later date.

About a year after the registration system was introduced, a pharmacy module was added. This module keeps track of the medications prescribed for each patient, and automatically enters the appropriate charges into the patient billing system.

Although these systems support the administrative functions in the hospital, a growing group of young physicians and nurses have been lobbying for a computer system to support clinical functions; one that will help them in managing the delivery of appropriate health care for their patients.

A STATE-OF-THE-ART SYSTEM

Dr. Norman Kornwitz, an orthopedic surgeon, was an especially strong advocate of a clinical information system. At a medical staff meeting, the group of physicians in attendance listened while Kornwitz described an impressive system he had seen on a recent trip to a professional meeeting in Boston.

"Let me give you an example of how the on-line system at Eastern General is used," Kornwitz said. "Several of us were observing open-heart surgery on a 60-year-old woman," he began. "The surgical team included five doctors, three nurses, and two heart-lung machine technicians. At 1:02 p.m. the heart-lung machine was stopped. The heart, which had not beaten for more than one hour while the operation was in progress, once again began to pump blood to the lungs and body.

"To be sure that her heart and lungs were functioning properly, it was necessary to take a blood sample. In fact, since the surgery began four and a half hours earlier this would be the seventh such sample taken.

"The nurse brought the blood sample to the dumbwaiter located in the operating room," continued Kornwitz, "and it was sent one floor up to the acute care laboratory. When it arrived, a buzzer rang and a technician immediately began the blood test.

"By 1:10 the tests were finished and the results were sent by computer to the operating room. A video display terminal located in the operating room beeped. The physicians looked at the monitor and read the lab results. The patient's condition was satisfactory.

"If you consider," continued Kornwitz, "that the time between drawing the sample and receiving the results was just eight minutes, this is about half the time it takes us to do the same thing. Right now the technicians in our acute care laboratory use an intercom or telephone to communicate the results to the operating room and other departments. Sometimes these lab results are difficult to get in an emergency situation. Doctors and nurses are often too busy treating a patient to answer the telephone.

"At Eastern General those problems have been eliminated. The results arrive as soon at the tests are finished. In fact the director of their acute care lab told me that the system has decreased errors and reduced stress in the lab, operating room, and patient care areas.

"While I have just described how their system is used in the operating room," Kornwitz concluded, "they also use it to collect health care data at its source and deliver the data where they are needed. What we need is to get chemistry results, pathology reports, X-ray reports, patient histories, prescriptions, and even request the delivery of a patient's chart right from the terminal. It's ineffecient, costly, and not in the best interest of the patient to have the information retrieval process rely on a people as we do. Paper reports pile up and become impossible to find, telephones go unanswered, and staff workers go tracking down reports from one lab to the next."

Although there was some disagreement about the type of information such a system should provide, it was agreed that the hospital needed to do something. The physicians at the meeeting decided to prepare a memo for distribution to the head of hospital administration and the director of MIS.

MANAGEMENT RESPONSE

The hospital administrator, Karen Miller, and the director of MIS, Bud Shaffer, agreed that something should be done. Miller asked Shaffer if one of his staff could prepare a report which identified possible projects, their costs and priorities.

Several weeks later such a report was submitted and Miller decided to focus first on a laboratory system, much like the one Kornwitz had described at Eastern General. To develop the system, Vista hired Meducomp, a software development company located in Dallas.

USER INVOLVEMENT

After these actions were taken, and during a medical staff meeting, Kornwitz expressed his frustration to his collegues. "This system will cost a bundle of money and I have serious doubts that it will be of much use," he said. "First, the administration has been working primarily with the MIS group, and second, they have farmed out the actual design work to a company in Dallas. When I asked about Eastern General's system, what impressed me was that the medical, nursing, and technical staff were heavily involved in its development. They made sure, at each step in the development process, that the system met their needs. The way we're going about it, the development of the system is out of our hands. Sure, that will interfere less with our busy life now -- but I think the physicians and staff who will use the system will suffer in the long run."

Fay Love, another physician at the meeting, added her concern. "From what you described, Norman, the system at Eastern was designed by the hospital's MIS staff. Doesn't it make more sense to have our staff develop the system? From what I have heard about Meducomp, they sell the same software system to every hospital, with few modifications. Doesn't it make more sense to develop one specifically to meet our own needs?"

Love suggested that Miller come to the next meeting. "In fact," she went on, "since she's the person in charge, I think she should consider taking a step back and appointing a committee of physicians, nurses, technicians, administrators, and MIS professionals. I agree that without this representation the system may prove disappointing.

QUESTIONS

1. Describe the difference between a hospital's administrative and clinical information systems.
2. What applications does the computer at Vista now support?
3. What applications can a clinical system support?
4. How would you describe the objectives of the new system?
5. The scope of a project relates to its range or ambition. Would you say that the scope of this project is narrow or wide? Explain.
6. When a new system is proposed it must be determined if the technical aspects of the system (hardware and software) are feasible or within the current capabilities of computer technologies. Is there anything in this case that suggests that the proposal would not be feasible?

7. How should the project proceed? Should Miller continue the progress she has already made, or should a team of physicians, nurses, administrators, and MIS professionals start from scratch? Why?
8. Do you think it would be best for the development of the system to focus on one application, or should several be developed in parallel?
9. At what point in the development of this system must preliminary cost data be estimated and tentative schedules be drawn?
10. Although the benefits of an administrative system include lower or contained operating costs, how would you measure the benefits of a clinical system?
11. When the requirements of a system are being reviewed during the development of a project, facts are collected from many sources including end-users. These facts will help define how the system will be or should be used. How would you go about collecting these facts?
12. Do you think custom tailored software developed by the MIS staff is the only reasonable way to proceed?
13. What should be the next step in this project?
14. Outline the steps that should be taken in the development of this system.
15. What role should general management play in the development of the system?

CHILD SUPPORT AGENCY

The workload was up, costs were increasing, and the collection record continued to be poor. The State Child Support Agency in this midwestern state was in jeopardy of losing its federal funding unless it improved its performance.

The Agency is responsible for enforcing the collection of funds from the absent parent and placing those payments into the hands of the custodial parent. And the state has a vested interest in these payments; unless the absent parent makes these child support payments, the custodial parent will likely show up on the state welfare roles.

NEW AUTOMATION PROJECT

Although the Child Support Agency does use word processing, it is less automated that most other state agencies. Jill Davenport, director of the agency, has concluded that the only logical step to improve office productivity, increase collections, and provide better management control over the collection process is to embark on an ambitious automation program.

At a meeting with Bob Jackson, the Director of the Department of Human Services and Davenport's boss, Davenport explained that her project should be given high priority since the benfits would likely far exceed development costs, and besides, they needed the system to continue to be eligible for federal assistance.

The Director of Human Services sent a memo to the state MIS department requesting a feasibility study. The MIS department employs over 200 programmers and analysts, and is responsible for supporting a range of applications used by various state agencies from tax collection to motor vehicles.

MIS SOLUTION: A CUSTOM DESIGNED SYSTEM

The state MIS goup is considered a COBOL shop: All of their applications are written in COBOL, a third generation computer language developed to support business applications.

Two months after the request was made, two systems analysts arrived at the Child Support Agency to study its needs. They began by talking with Davenport in an effort to carefully define the problem. They learned that current methods and procedures were inefficient, and that it was not only difficult to keep up with the paperwork requirements, but that the system was ineffectual in supporting the agency's primary function, to enforce the collection of child support payments.

The systems analysts concluded that the objective of a new system should be to automate the paperwork process so that forms could be automatically completed, and to be useful in the process of locating missing parents, establishing paternity, preparing the paperwork for court appearances, and supporting and enforcing the collection process.

But the system would be limited in scope, and would not be capable of making inquiries to other systems, such as motor vehicle bureaus, in other states in an effort to find an absent parent. This feature might be added at a later time.

To learn more about the way that the agency operated, the systems analysts observed the processing of cases from the moment they entered the system through the process of collection and payment to the custodial parent. The analysts read training manuals and documented procedures which the staff followed, interviewed staff members, and collected samples of the documents which they had to prepare.

Once back in MIS headquarters, the systems analysts began to analyze the facts they had collected. They drew data flow diagrams which documented the flow of data within the current system. And they began to talk about the costs of designing and programming a new system.

COMMERCIAL SOFTWARE PACKAGE

While the MIS group was preparing a preliminary report, one of the staff in the Child Support Agency, Phil Drake, returned from a professional meeting with information about a commercial software package developed by a major computer company expressly for child support agencies.

The package was written in a fourth generation computer language, and its developer claimed that users could "talk" to the system in plain English rather than computer jargon. Thanks to this approach, programs can be tailored so that they would fit in with the operations as they now exist. Screens can be customized to incorporate whatever codes are currently used. For example, an absent parent can be identified as AP (Absent Parent), AB (ABsent), or AF (Absent Father). Reports can be customized to provide just the information the user requires, and terminology in those reports can reflect the terminology used at the agency.

As the brochure stated, "Particular attention is given to those problem areas which may impede the primary goals of establishing support orders and increasing collections." To meet these objectives the software includes several different modules.

CASE SETUP

The first module, Case Setup, is used when a case is first entered into the system. A case can be opened by referral under the provision of Title IV-A of the Social Security Act, or by the application of the custodial parent. In either situation, the system's Case Setup module provides the screens necessary to enter the relevant data.

ABSENT PARENTS

After the case has been set up, one of the first steps is to determine the whereabouts of the absent parent. If this information is not provided in the original referral, then the systems provide a mechanism to cross check and determine if the absent parent appears in any other cases, and if so, whether his or her whereabouts are known. If the absent parent is still not located, information may be requested from outside sources, such as agencies in other states or motor vehicle databases. When the whereabouts of the absent parent are determined, this data becomes part of the case record.

ESTABLISHING PATERNITY

It is often necessary to determine who is actually responsible for child support. Using this system, inquiries can be made of hospital records, and the necessary forms can be generated to compel court-ordered blood tests. When paternity is established this data becomes part of the updated case record.

SUPPORT OBLIGATIONS

After paternal responsibility for child support has been established, but no court order for support exists, the system can be used to proceed with the establishment of a legal financial obligation. The system can automatically request dates for interviews, schedule appointments, and generate legal documents.

ENFORCING AND COLLECTING SUPPORT OBLIGATIONS

Even after the court or appropriate agency orders support, it will still be necessary to monitor and perhaps enforce that support. Through the use of automatic case reviews, the staff will learn if regular payments are being made. If not, special reports will alert the staff to take the necessary action. Then requests can be made for the system to generate the necessary forms to assign wages, intercept tax refunds, or execute other enforcement strategies.

MANAGMENT INFORMATION

The system also provides management information. Because it monitors case activity, workloads can be monitored, case loads can be adjusted, agency-wide priorities can be set, and ad hoc reports can be prepared quickly.

When Drake described this system to Davenport, he made it clear that it would be foolish to let the MIS group proceed with a system that probably wouldn't measure up to this commercial package. "This commercial software can be up and running in just a few months, and we will know exactly what it will cost -- in contrast to the MIS department, which always delivers late and over budget."

Davenport, on the other hand, knew that MIS preferred to develop their own software. She was reluctant to interfere with the development of the system at this time.

QUESTIONS

1. What does the Child Support Agency do?
2. Are they using a computer system? Explain.
3. Why do they need a new system?
4. What is the difference between a custom system developed by the MIS department and a commercial system?
5. Describe the steps followed by the MIS department in conducting a preliminary study of the proposed system.
6. A preliminary study must focus on user requirements. Do you think this focus was taken by the MIS department? Explain any changes you might suggest.
7. Describe the features of the commercial system.
8. What problems can be minimized if a commercial system is used?
9. What arguments can be made to favor the development of a custom system?
10. Which system do you think would better meet the needs of the agency? Support your answer.
11. Why is Davenport reluctant to suggest that MIS consider this commercial system?
12. How would you proceed if you were director of the agency?

SOX INC.

Sox Inc. is a leading manufacturer and distributor of women's hosiery. The company quickly gained market dominance several years ago when it revolutionized the way in which hosiery was packaged, distributed, and sold.

Sox's product is attractively packaged in a square plastic container. Although in the past hosiery was primarily sold in department and specialty stores, Sox began selling its product through point-of-purchase displays located in the high-traffic areas of supermarkets and drugstores. This strategy worked exceptionally well. Within a few years, it achieved a 45 percent market share of all hosiery sales.

Also contributing to Sox's success is the way that it distributes its product. Instead of relying on drugstore and supermarket clerks to place reorders with wholesalers, Sox employs a sales staff that travels to each retail location. These salespeople, assigned to one of five distribution centers across the country, drive vans that hold enough inventory to service the accounts on their route. The vans are actually warehouses on wheels. As a result, Sox also does not have to rely on the retail store clerks to keep the display stocked.

When the drivers arrive at a store, they see what stock is needed, go back to their vans, pull the items from the storage shelves, return to the store, and replenish the display. Then they fill out the paperwork, leave a copy with the store, keep one copy for themselves, and send a third copy to corporate headquarters in Atlanta using an overnight delivery service. Upon their arrival in Atlanta, the data are entered into key-to-disk machines and the central computer is updated in the batch mode. Shortly thereafter invoices are mailed to the stores.

GROWTH PROBLEMS

Sox has been extremely successful using these methods. Although several other competitors have tried to imitate Sox, few have achieved even a small market share. To ensure this market leadership position, Sox periodically introduces new products, most of them targeted to the fashion-conscious consumer. Because new products tend to be introduced into the line faster than old ones are dropped, the total number of items in the line is steadily increasing.

As this number increases, so does the problem of inventory control. With more products, a greater range of items must be carried in the vans. And as the sales of each product line also increase, the vans have to carry more of all items.

Recently the marketing department announced a new fashion line of hosiery. Production, it said, would begin within two months. The corporate distribution manager, Cassandra Williams, learned of these plans at a department heads meeting. At the meeting she was quick to point out that the vans could not possibly accommodate this increase, as they were already filled to capacity.

THE DISTRIBUTION SOLUTION

Shortly after this meeting, Williams wrote a memo recommending that the corporation phase out its conventional vans (in which there was not enough room for a person to stand erect) and begin to acquire larger step vans (in which a person can stand). She explained that the new vans would have enough room to accommodate the new product line and would eliminate the crowded conditions in the conventional vans. She went on to say that this might help reverse a decline in driver productivity that had been plaguing the company over the last two years.

THE DATA PROCESSING SOLUTION

Chan Lee also learned of the new product line at the department heads meeting. Lee, manager of corporate MIS, stayed out of the discussion because he felt that this was strictly a distribution problem: If Williams got her step vans, then the problem would be solved. But later that day it suddenly occurred to Lee that Sox did not have a distribution problem at all; it had a data processing problem.

The next morning Lee asked Williams if she could wait three weeks before taking any further action. She agreed.

During this time Lee met with his senior systems analyst, the manager of inventory control, and two route drivers. After collecting many facts from them, he began to formulate a solution to the capacity problem. Bringing this group together at a meeting, he began to unfold his plans.

"We already have historical sales data in our database for every product sold in every point-of-purchase display. The key to my idea is to use these data more effectively.

"Suppose," he continued, "that we generate a statistical forecast from the data. Take the Speedy Suprette location in Chattanooga as an example. The database might show that during the two-week period before the last visit, 25 pairs of our `sheer brite' line were sold. In the two-week period before this restocking trip, the database might show that 22 pairs were sold. And in the two-week period before that trip, it might show that 19 pairs were sold. This averages 22 pairs for the two-week period over the last three restocking trips. We could then use this average as the statistical forecast of the number of pairs we would have expected to sell since the most recent restocking trip."

"But I still don't see how this forecast would be used and how it would save storage space in our vans," said Chuck Wilson, a van driver who had been with the company for six years.

"When a driver is scheduled to service a point-of-purchase display," explained Lee, "the distribution center closest to the driver's home base will produce a forecast from its database. This forecast will be used to estimate the demand since the last restocking trip. Next, the software will use this forecast to compute the quantity of each product to be included in a shrink-wrapped package. The computer will then print a picking document for the warehouse and also produce the paperwork for the driver, including an invoice to leave with the retailer. When the shipping department receives the picking document, it will pick the order, package it, and send it to the shipping dock."

"I'm beginning to understand," interrupted Gail Newsome, the senior systems analyst. "The drivers wouldn't have to keep a large stock of each product. They'd only carry prepackaged orders. And when they arrived at the retailer's location, they'd simply bring in the prepackaged order, unwrap it, stock the shelves, and give the paperwork to the store manager." Newsome paused. "But I see one major flaw in your system."

"What's that?"

"The package the driver delivers might not have the right number of items. In other words, actual sales since the last restocking trip might differ from our statistical forecast. So, the stock in the package for a particular point-of-service display might be more or less than is needed to restock the shelves."

Lee had thought about this problem, too. "The driver would actually use all of the items in the prepack. There would, of course, be times when it included too few items. Then it would not be possible to restock the shelves to the desired levels. And there would also be times when too many items would be included, and the shelves would hold more than was actually needed. But I don't think this would create a serious problem.

"What is important," Lee continued, "is that the driver complete an exception report. In this report, the driver would enter the amount by which the prepack includes too many or too few of an item. When the prepack includes the right amount, no entry will be necessary in the report. In this case, the forecast would have been perfect."

Lee then explained that each of the drivers would be issued specialized portable computers. At the end of the day, they would enter their exception reports for each point-of-purchase display and send these data through the telephone network to the district distribution center. At the distribution center, the data would automatically be entered into the database and would update the demand for the most recent period, so that when a forecast was prepared for the next delivery period, it would be computed using accurate demand data.

Although Lee was convinced that the plan was technically feasible, he was not sure of the economics, so he asked the group if they would help him prepare a developmental budget and an estimate of the savings that such a system would produce.

A week later they submitted a report showing that the system would cost approximately $4 million. This would include the computers needed by the drivers, new minicomputers at the five distribution centers, an increase in the storage capacity of the corporate mainframe, software development costs, and communications equipment needed to interface the portable computers with the minicomputers at the distribution centers.

They estimated that at a minimum, 73 data entry personnel would no longer be needed to enter the data supplied by the drivers. These drivers would now enter their own exception data through portable computers in the field. In addition, the company would no longer need to spend several million dollars on new step vans. And another significant advantage would be an improvement of approximately two days in cash flow, because the retailers would now receive their bills when the order was delivered rather than waiting several days for the bill to arrive from Atlanta.

Their analysis suggested a rate of return on the investment of about 80 percent, and since most of the firm's projects produced a rate of return in the vicinity of 20 percent, they felt this project was a particularly attractive one. Furthermore, their estimates did not include the value that management would receive from access to a timely database that could be used for better control over operations, so the return would be even higher.

Lee was prepared to recommend that the project be completed in three stages. In the first stage, only the Atlanta district would be converted to the new system. If the results of this pilot study met expectations, then the second stage would be a conversion of the eastern divisions. Finally, the rest of the divisions in the country would be converted.

QUESTIONS

1. Write a short paragraph that defines Sox's problem.
2. How would you describe the objectives of the proposed computer system?
3. Does the project suggest a broad or a narrow scope? Explain.
4. Do you feel this system is technically feasible? Describe any concerns you might have.
5. What costs did the group consider in its preliminary estimate? What benefits did it identify? Do you think it overlooked any costs or benefits?

6. Do you think that Lee's preliminary schedule is reasonable? Would you recommend that the entire project be completed in one stage rather than three? Explain.
7. If you were to manage this project, who would you include on the team that analyzes the system? Would you include a route driver? Why?
8. What types of facts might be collected in the detailed study of this system? How might these facts be obtained?
9. Do you think it would be necessary to develop custom-tailored software to implement this application? Explain.
10. Compare the solutions proposed by Williams and by Lee's group. Which one would you recommend? Why?
11. What should be the next step?
12. What role should general management play in this project?

D M V

"Why can't we go back to our old system? At least we know it works! Maybe it can get us out of this mess." Bill Maloney, the state's attorney general, was on the phone with Mark Bridger. Bridger, the director of the Department of Motor Vehicles (DMV), was doing his best to cope with a crisis that was becoming worse by the hour.

Two months earlier, the state began using a new data processing system designed to streamline operations at the DMV. Although the cutover -- direct conversion -- to the new system was without incident, problems began to mount soon after the system was placed in operation.

Now the system was unable to cope with the workload. More than a million drivers had been unable to register their cars. To make the situation even worse, many of those who registered their cars after the system went into operation were incorrectly listed in the database as operating unregistered vehicles. And renewal notices -- issued automatically by the new computer system -- had been sent to the wrong drivers. In fact, so many drivers had been forced to drive without a registration that the attorney general, Bill Maloney, had ordered the state police to cease citing drivers for this offense. No one, it seemed, had been spared: Even some of the vehicles operated by public works departments and local police forces throughout the state were registered to the wrong municipalities!

BACKGROUND

When the system was first conceived, a little over three years ago, the DMV expressed a need for a more up-to-date information-processing system than the ten-year-old system it was using. The DMV especially needed a system with a strong DBMS, to have more flexibility in accessing data and in making changes in the application software. Its current system used a conventional file-management approach.

In addition to performing all of the routine record-keeping functions such as maintaining automobile registration data, the DMV wanted the new system to automatically notify the state's five million drivers of license and registration renewals. It also wanted the system to be capable of allowing updates of the state's rating surcharge database to be made on a daily basis. This surcharge database keeps track of violation points against individual drivers and is used to penalize bad drivers by making them pay higher insurance rates. Under the old system, this database was updated periodically, but it was not unusual -- due to inefficient update procedures -- for the driver's record to be updated as much as three or four months after the conviction took place.

POLITICAL FACTORS

When the idea for a new computer system was originally suggested to the governor, he agreed that an effort such as this was long overdue. But he was not pleased to hear that it would take five years to develop and bring the project into full operation. It is alleged that he then asked DMV director Bridger to find a consulting firm to develop the system in two years so that the completed system would be finished in time to be used during his reelection campaign as an example of his administration's accomplishments.

THE CONSULTANTS

Shortly after the governor's alleged request to expedite the development of the system, Bridger met with the information services division of Driscol and Russell, one of the country's leading public accounting firms. After studying the project's objectives, the manager of this division, Mike Price, suggested that the only way it could be completed in two years would be to use a fourth generation language.

"We will still use a structured approach and build the system in modules," explained Price, "but the 4GL will save us a lot of time in programming, debugging, and testing the project."

Bridger was impressed with Price's confidence in his firm's ability to deliver the needed software and, above all, to deliver it on time. Within three months a $6.5 million contract was signed with Driscol and Russell.

The software development process went smoothly for the DMV. The senior systems analyst for Driscol and Russell spent six weeks at the DMV, during which time he learned about the current system and the characteristics of the new one. Once the systems analysis was complete and a preliminary plan approved, Driscol and Russell had few interactions with the DMV. According to the senior systems analyst at Driscol and Russell, the DMV preferred it this way, as the DMV was already overburdened with day-to-day problems.

THE SYSTEM FAILS

The system was delivered right on schedule, and during the first few weeks, as the workload on the new system increased, it seemed to perform well. Data entry was made from on-line terminals, and users found the system efficient. As might be expected at the start, those who used the system complained a little about the new procedures, but no serious problems emerged.

But as more and more new tasks were added to the system, the operators began to report an increase in response time. When the system was finally in full operation, the response time became intolerable. At best, response times were in the five-to-eight second range and frequently took as long as one to two minutes. The original contract specified that response times were to be no longer than three to five seconds.

An increase in response time, however, was just the tip of the iceberg. First, it was not possible to process all of the jobs on the new system. Even an increase to a 24-hour operation was insufficient to update the database. Within a few months, the backlog grew to such proportions that 1.4 million automobile registrations had not been processed. Meanwhile, when police stopped cars that did not have valid registrations, the drivers were arrested. As the protest from drivers began to mount, the attorney general's office stepped in and ordered the police to stop making arrests for invalid registrations.

Then an even more dramatic problem surfaced. It slowly became apparent that the database was contaminated with bad data, that the automobile registrations listed the wrong owners.

STATE DEPARTMENT OF DATA PROCESSING

With the system in total chaos, the DMV director and the attorney general decided to call in Gail Hendrix, the director of the state department of data processing. Hendrix had known about this project since its inception, when she had been appalled not only that her department had been frozen out of the development process but that the bid had apparently gone to a company without the usual competitive bidding process.

Hendrix was not surprised at the DMV's problems. During her first meeting with Bridger and Maloney, she shed some light on the sources of the problem. "I can't understand why Driscol and Russell used PROWRITE. Everyone knew it was a new 4GL, that it had lots of bugs to be worked out, and that no one had really tested it on a large project yet. Not only that, but PROWRITE was developed to run smaller MIS jobs. I don't think it was even meant to run transaction jobs where the system must handle several transactions per second."

Bridger asked, "How would you have developed the system?"

Hendrix replied, "I think COBOL should have been used for those modules that did the heavy processing. Then a 4GL, but not PROWRITE, could have been used for some of the other modules, especially the report-writing ones."

FINDING A SOLUTION

At the meeting with Hendrix and Bridger, Maloney insisted that they come up with a solution. "We've got our motor vehicle system in a shambles. To solve the problem tomorrow is even too late. What are we going to do?"

Bridger was in favor of holding a meeting with Driscol and Russell to determine what they could do to straighten out the situation. "Perhaps they could rewrite some of the transaction modules in COBOL, as Hendrix suggested."

Hendrix felt differently. "They've lost their credibility with me. I think we should write this software off as a complete loss and begin the development of a new system here in our own DP organization."

Maloney, however, was certainly not satisfied. "Look, why can't we bring our old system back into operation? At least we'll get the public and the politicians off our back."

"Bill, you asked me that on the phone last week, and I told you that it would take months to get the old software running again," replied Bridger. "And besides, we developed this new system to solve problems that our old software couldn't. I don't think yours is a reasonable solution."

QUESTIONS

1. Describe the DMV's problem.
2. What are the guidelines and techniques that should be used in the system development process? To what extent do you think Driscol and Russell followed them?
3. What were the new system's objectives? Were they reasonable?
4. How was the tentative schedule for the system's development established?
5. How does technical feasibility play a role in this project?
6. Is there any evidence to suggest that the detailed analysis phase of the development process was neglected?
7. Describe what is meant by "breaking a system into modules." Can you describe one module that might be found in the system?
8. Give an example of one output required by the users at the DMV.
9. Give an example of an input.
10. Is it suggested that data entry in the new system is on line or off-line? Explain the difference.
11. Do you think that source data automation could solve any of DMV's problems?

12. Describe, in very general terms, the use of files in this system.
13. Is there any evidence that inadequate system controls contributed to the DMV's problems?
14. What is the difference between a 4GL and COBOL? Do you think it was a bad choice to use a 4GL? Why?
15. Do you think that using a prototype in the development process would have saved the DMV from disaster?
16. What type of conversion strategy was followed? Which would you have recommended? Why?
17. Where in the development process would you place the blame for this system's failure?
18. If you were the DMV director, what would you recommend as the next step?
19. With increasing frequency, companies with larger DP backlogs are turning to outside sources for help in developing applications. Using the insight gained from this case, what precautions would you take to minimize the kinds of problems that the DMV suffered?

COMMUNICATIONS AND DISTRIBUTED DATA PROCESSING

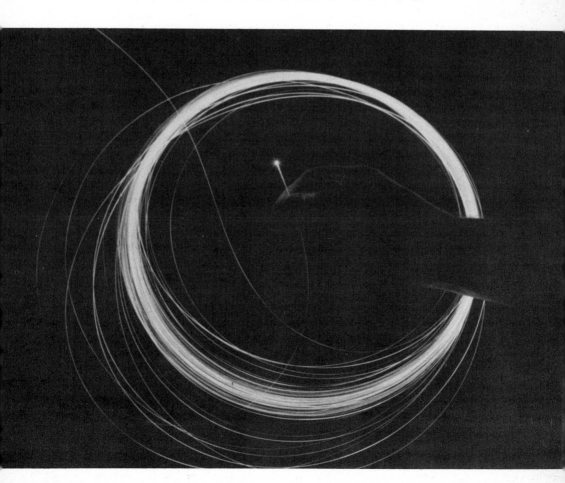

Communication systems consist of the hardware and software that links computers with terminals, printers, and other computers. Many different types of links and configurations are possible, some of which are described in the cases of this section. One of the most fundamental distinctions to draw is whether a system supports centralized or distributed data processing. With **centralized data processing**, the computer, storage devices, software, and data processing staff are all located in one central facility, even though the users may work at distant terminals. **Distributed data processing** places the computers, storage devices, and even some data processing staff in separate locations throughout the organization, with the object of providing a computer system that is more responsive to its users' needs.

Five cases involving communications and distributed data processing are presented in this section. The first, Checkers Pizza Inc., deals with a firm seeking to handle a large volume of data and provide timely management information through installation of local area networks (LANs). In the second case, Citizens Bank and Trust, recently merged from two banks, confronts the issues of centralized versus distributed data processing. Metropolitan College, in the third case, examines the possibility of linking all classrooms and dormitory rooms together in a new computer network. In the fourth case a law firm, O'brien and Gonsalves, finds that the data-sharing that proves awkward or impossible with their stand-alone micros would be straightforward with a local area network. The final case, Wast Inc., also concerns data sharing, in this case using a token ring topology.

CHECKERS PIZZA INC.

Gail Dawson was nervous. She was about to begin her presentation to the board of directors at Checkers Pizza. In a few minuites she would describe the results of her feasibility study and recommend that the company embark on an extensive development program that she believed would give them a competitive edge over other pizza chains.

COMPANY BACKGROUND

Checkers Pizza, started fifteen years ago as a regional chain, now has over 3000 stores and is growing rapidly. Sales this year were nearly $1.5 billion. Within five years they expect to have 10,000 franchises in their network.

Built on a marketing concept of home delivery, the chain has been very successful. In advertising campaigns, Checkers promises a pizza delivered to your door in less than 30 minutes. And because of this convienience factor and the trend toward eating out more often, the order phones are ringing off the hook.

ORDER PROCESSING PROBLEMS

But success has brought problems, one of which is the fact that it is difficult for the stores to efficiently handle as many as one million telephone orders each week. Compounding the problem is the fact that the chain now has several stores in most metropolitan areas. In these areas customers do not necessarily call the store closest to where they live or work, and in some cases customers call a store that doesn't even deliver to their neighborhood. Although some customers who call the wrong store will redial another number, others probably call a competitor.

Three months ago, the president, Randy Johnson, asked Gail Dawson, corporate MIS director, to study the possibility of using computers to help in the ordering process. Dawson, with two others from her department, decided to take a fresh look at the problem and not be bound by any of the procedures, manual or computer, that were currently in use. Now it was time to present her results to the board of directors.

NEW PROPOSAL

Dawson began her presentation with a brief overview of the current problem. Then she began to unveil her proposal.

"I'm going to recommend an integrated network of computers that will include a **local area network** of micros at each store, minicomputers located at ten metropolitan centers throught the company, and finally, a minicomputer here at headquarters.

"The local area networks will include **point-of-sale terminals** that will be used as cash registers. In addition, the networks will include printers and also several micros that will support accounting, inventory, and payroll applications for each store."

She went on to explain that the networks in those stores that are geographically separated from any other store in the chain will be directly tied into the corporate minicomputer through a computer which is called a gateway. But when there is more than one store in a metropolitan area, then the store's LAN will be tied through a gateway to a regional telemarketing center. And it will be these telemarketing centers that will solve many of the ordering problems Checkers has today.

TELEMARKETING CENTERS

The telemarketing centers would be staffed by trained salespeople. Unlike the situation at a local store where someone at the counter answers the phone, the telemarketing sales staff would be trained to take orders. Here is how the new system would work.

Customers in a metropolitan area will have just one number to call, the telemarketing center. The phone will be answered by a telemarketing salesperson, and the order -- including the person's name, address, and telephone number -- will be directly entered into a terminal.

The terminals will be microcomputers connected in a local area network. The network will also have a microcomputer that will function as a **file server**, the purpose of which is to manage the data stored on the network's central hard disk.

Once the customer data have been entered, the data will be sent over the local network to the file server, where the customer's telephone number will be used to search the database and find the closest store serving that customer's exchange. Next, the order data are automatically sent from a bridge over private lines leased from the telephone company to the bridge at the local store, where the order then enters the store's LAN and is sent to the printer, which prints the order.

MANAGEMENT INFORMATION SYSTEM

"The transaction order sytem will also serve as the foundation for a Management Information System," continued Dawson. "Each evening the micros at the stores can poll the point-of-sale terminals, update the database, and produce several sales reports that can show the local managers how the store is doing.

"Headquarters, too, will be able to poll the local stores and obtain summary sales data that will provide useful information for planning and control over operations," Dawson went on. "For example, they will be able to see the results of advertising campaigns almost instantly. As things stand now, we have to wait weeks before the sales data come in from the field."

BENEFITS AND COST

"There will be many benefits from the system," she explained. "Customers won't have to dial two numbers to find the store closest to them, and their orders will be taken by trained salespeople. We also suspect that these trained sales order people will boost the average sale from $10 to $12 by suggesting drinks, deserts, and promoting specials, for example.

"In addition, we can use the system to track customer complaints and even maintain a file of customers who have given us bad checks, so that when they call for another order we can require cash payment.

"As you can imagine," continued Dawson, "the cost of the system will be high. Each store will require about $10,000 worth of equipment. Each telemarketing center will require another $40,000 worth, and we would have to spend about $90,000 here at headquarters. Furthermore, we will have to lease telemarketing facilities and maintain a staff at the telemarketing centers which will include a manager and 12 to 100 agents. And these are only estimates."

QUESTIONS

1. Write a brief paragraph describing Checkers' problem.
2. Describe the proposed system.
3. What is a local area network? How would it be used by the staff and management at the local stores?
4. What piece of hardware would be used at the local store to connect the local area network with the corporate minicomputer?

5. Over what communications media would the store's network communicate with the telemarketing centers?
6. How would the terminals be used at the telemarketing centers?
7. What is a file server? How will it be used in the telemarketing centers?
8. What function does a bridge serve in a local network? How will it be used in this case?
9. In some situations a computer information system can give an organization a competitive advantage. Do you think this is an example of such a situation? Is this system justified?
10. If the go-ahead is given, what role do you think management should play in the development of this system? Who are the end-users? What role, if any, would they play in development of the system?

CITIZENS BANK AND TRUST

Within three years after the state passed a banking law allowing banks to operate branches in other states, Citizens Bank and Trust, one of the largest banks in the region, anounced a merger with Bank Southeast, a bank that ranked about 20th in the region.

For the first year after the merger was finalized, the banks operated independently of one another; but in the last few months, with bank profits under pressure, the president of Citizens has begun to look at ways to integrate operations and services.

TWO BANKS, TWO COMPUTER SYSTEMS

One of the first areas he turned to was the computer information network. Both banks depend heavily on computers. Citizens maintained an IBM mainframe that supported 400 teller teminals, 1300 automatic teller machines, and another 100 terminals used by the accounting department, loan department, audit department, and professional staff.

At Southeast, a DEC VAX superminicomputer was used to support 100 tellers, 53 automatic teller machines, and another 25 terminals used by the accounting, loan, and audit departments and the professional staff.

The MIS staff at Citizens included a vice-president of corporate computing, eight MIS managers, and a staff of 40 programmer/analysts. They are reponsible for writing new software, maintaining and modifying the old software, and supporting end-user requirements.

The MIS staff at Southeast includes a director of DP and a staff of 12 programmer/analysts who maintain and modify the software which the bank had purchased from a computer software firm. Few programs were developed from scratch by this group.

ALTERNATIVES FOR A NEW SYSTEM

To gain some insight on the problem, the president of Citizens called a meeting. Included among those invited were Citizen's vice-president of corporate computing, Southeast's director of DP, and a consultant who had been recommended by a colleague at a recent professional meeting.

The vice-president of corporate computing at Citizens, Alfred Young, known for being very outspoken, confidently opened the meeting. "The duplication of data processing efforts has never made much sense to us here at Citizens," he said. "What we need to do is consolidate all data processing activities to our central location. Once they are centralized, we will be better able to maintain control of the data processing network and in addition we will be spreading our operating costs over a bigger operation. This will improve our productivity, which as you know hasn't been as good as it should be."

Fred Markley of Southeast quickly became defensive. "That solution will cost a fortune," Markley said. "You'll need private communication lines from our terminals to your central facilities. Leasing them from the telephone company will cost you more than you will save by shutting us down. And if you centralize your system, you'll lose touch with the needs we have at Southeast. Our operation is different from yours, and to impose your methods and procedures on us would be a mistake."

Tension was high. It was clear that Markley's job was on the line. An expanded centralized facility would have little room for him, certainly nothing comparable to the current position he held at Southeast.

DISTRIBUTED DATA PROCESSING

Bonnie Hendrix, the consultant, offered a different solution to the problem. Her suggestion would drastically change the computing environment not only at Citizens' centralized facility but at all branches including the new acquisition. Hendrix explained that the bank should move to a **distributed data processing** environment, one in which a good share of the processing would not be carried out centrally but would occur at the branches themselves. She said that the costs of minicomputers had come down enough so that it made sense to place minicomputers at each of the branches, and to assign all local processing demands to these machines. That would mean that demand deposits, savings accounts, and loan processing would all occur in the branches. The only functions that might be centralized would be automatic teller machine processing, bank accounting, payroll, and personnel functions.

Hendrix went on to describe how this would be the only sensible way to proceed. With this strategy, she explained, new branches could be added to the system, and since they would be resposible for supporting much of their own processing needs, the resources of the central computer would not be overburdened with the additions.

Young was not happy with this solution. "How can we put computer resources in the hands of a branch manager who probably knows little if anything about computers? And we would lose control. With access to the system from hundreds of locations, and databases on every minicomputer, we would be a prime target for computer crime. Distributed environments are fine for factories or insurance companies, but not for us."

Hendrix replied that it might be necessary to assign a computer professional to some of the larger branches, but for the most part these branch systems would be run by the current staff at the bank. They would, of course, be properly trained, she added. And Hendrix wasn't too concerned with Young's remark about security. She said that adequate controls could be built into the system, and that many banks were moving to this type of computing environment.

Hendrix then went to the blackboard and sketched the new system. She pointed out how the distributed system could facilitate communication between banks. "Suppose a depositor with an account at the downtown location walks into one of your branch offices and needs to cash a check. The local computer would not find that customer's name in its depositor database and then would automatically refer to a directory maintained by the central computer. This directory would identify the branch at which records are kept, and would then initiate an automatic request for a balance verification from that branch. If the balance is sufficient to cash the check, then the balance would be updated and authorization to cash the check would be returned through the central computer to the branch at which the customer is waiting. This process would take but a few seconds.

"And your automatic teller system would work in much the same way," Hendrix went on. "All of the automatic tellers would be connected to the central computer. This, by the way, would provide Southeast's customers with access to their funds from Citizens' larger ATM network. Once a customer enters a password, the ATM system would reference the central directory and determine the branch at which the customer's account is held. Then the system would forward the request to the branch minicomputer, update the balance as long as sufficient funds are available to cover the check, and then return the authorization for a cash disbursement to the originating ATM."

At this point in the meeting it was clear that both Young and Markley were quite upset with the direction that the meeting had taken. The president decided to adjourn, and called another meeting next week.

QUESTIONS

1. What is a centralized sytem?
2. Describe distributed data processing.

3. What is the role of communications in a centralized system? In a distributed system?
4. How would a centrally managed company be affected by a changing to a distributed data processing system?
5. Some argue that a distributed system will bring the computing resources down to the level of end-users, the people who know best how a system needs to be used. This should thereby ensure a more productive and effective use of computer resources. Do you agree? Why or why not?
6. "The distributed sytem proposed by Hendrix would take the system out of the hands of centrally located information processing professionals." Do you agree or disagree with this statement?
7. Explain the positions taken by Markley and Young. How are they threatened by the proposal made by Hendrix? Explain.
8. What benefits do distributed systems bring to their users? What are their disadvantages?
9. How would the bank customers benefit from a decentralized solution?
10. Explain how computers in a distributed system can communicate with each other. Use the example, given in the case, of a customer making a withdrawal from a branch other than the one where his or her records are stored.
11. Would you say that the system proposed by Hendrix could be classified as a pure decentralized system, or are parts of the system centralized?
12. How do you think the role of centralized data processing would change in a decentralized environment? In many companies the change from a centralized to a decentralized operation causes the central staff to shrink in size Do you think this might happen at Citizens?
13. How do you think the staff at Southeast would be affected by a decentralized solution?
14. If you were the president of Citizens, how would you proceed at the next meeting?

METROPOLITAN COLLEGE

Located near Denver, Metropolitan College is a four-year school offering bachelor's degrees in liberal arts, business administration, and health care. Current enrollment includes 2350 full-time day students and 350 part-time evening students.

The computer has played a growing part in the curriculum over the last 10 years. While it has been used by the school's administration for accounting, payroll, student records, and course registration for almost 15 years, its use by some areas, such as English, psychology, and education, has been more recent. The business department has always been a heavy user of the system.

At present the school owns two DEC VAX super-minicomputers. One is used strictly for administrative computing and the other for academic computing.

Tied to the academic computer are 150 terminals located in clusters of 10 to 15 at various points around the campus. The largest cluster is in the school's library, and is available 7 days a week and 14 hours a day. The other clusters are open fewer days and for more limited hours.

INCREASED USE

Recently there has been an increase in the use of computer resources at Metropolitan College. The English department has required all students -- including those in freshman English -- to write their weekly compositions on the computers, and the psychology department is experimenting with computer-assisted education. They may computerize the entire statistics course which their majors are required to take.

Al Shire, the director of academic computing, has proposed a new **network** that that will link all classrooms and dormitory rooms -- about 65 percent of the full-time day students live in dorms -- to the DEC computer.

At a meeting with the vice-president of finance, Stuart Nailer, he explained how the system would work. The entire campus would be wired and plugs would be installed in every dorm room, classroom, and faculty office. To use the system a person would simply plug a microcomputer into the network.

"It seems to me that this would cost a lot of money and hardly give us any benefits over the way we do things now," was Stuart Nailer's response.

"That's not true at all," Shire said. "There are several advantages. First the students would have access to the school's academic computer around the clock, seven days a week."

"Wait a minute," interrupted Nailer. "You're assuming that every faculty member and student will have a microcomputer to plug into the network. That's totally unrealistic."

"I don't think so," Shire said, "because a recent study I completed showed that about 20 percent of our students own computers or rent them from the bookstores downtown. And I'm sure you've heard about some schools, like Grant Tech, that now require all freshmen to have a micro when they enroll for their first semester.

"But let's not get into that issue right now. Why don't I show you why I think the installation of a network makes a lot of sense as we plan the future of our academic computing services?"

SHARING THE LOAD

Shire explained that with a network a lot of the computing load can be downloaded from the DEC VAX. The VAX, while it was not used to capacity now, would be at that level in about two years. And to replace it with a larger computer would be very costly. Instead, a network could offload some of the computing requirements. For example, not only could students in a computer course write and test their programs on their micros, but students in the freshman English class could write their papers these machines as well. In fact, even if only 30 percent of the students use their micros, this will represent an enormous decrease in the burden placed on the VAX.

"And what I will also propose," continued Shire, "is that we install an **electronic mail system** in the network. With this system students will be able to send their finished homework automatically to their professor, and professors can route memos and homework directly to students. The administrative staff would also find this useful, and I would bet that the electronic mail system will reduce the costs in our campus mailroom."

"What kind of software and hardware would we need?" asked Nailer.

"Well, the big problem would be the cabling. Since the dorm rooms aren't even wired for telephones, we would have to start from scratch. And we have three choices. We can use shielded **twisted wire pair**, **coaxial cable**, or even **fiber optic cable**. Actually fiber optic cable would probably be too expensive for our purposes, and twisted wire pair might restrict us too much. Grant Tech used coaxial cables."

"Do we need to wire every computer directly to the VAX?" asked Nailer.

"No. We would probably use a hybrid star and ring topology. A **topology** is a physical map or layout of a network," he explained. "In a **star topology** each micro or device is tied directly to a microcomputer known as a **controller**. All the micros in a building, for example, would be linked to a controller. Then the controller in one physical location would be connected to a controller at another loation. The controllers connected in this way would represent a **ring topology**. Since both a star and ring toplogy would be used, we would say the network has a **hybrid topology**.

"In addition to the cabling," continued Shire, "we would also need network software. The software we have now wouldn't be capable of functioning in this environment -- we would need **multiuser software** so that a number of users could gain access to the system at the same time. And every computer in the network would need a network interface board that would be used with this new software so that the micros could interact with the network."

"Would the users need special training to use the network?" asked Nailer.

"No. The software would take the reponsibility of initiating any instructions necessary to interact with the other computers on the netwoork. When the student or professor used the network, he or she would not be aware of the interface with the other equipment. It would be a `seamless' process."

"Al, it sounds like we might be interested, but the big issue will be cost, I'm afraid. How about coming up with some figures, and then we can talk about this again."

QUESTIONS

1. What is a network?
2. Is the current sytem used at Metropolitan College a distributed system?
3. Explain the current system.
4. Describe the system that Shire proposes.
5. What is meant by the topolgy of a network? Explain the proposed topolgy at Metropolitan.
6. Why is cabling an issue? What are the alternatives?
7. How would the students and faculty benefit from the proposed system?
8. How could the proposed system postpone the need to expand the DEC VAX central superminicomputer?
9. What are the disadvantages of switching to the proposed network?
10. Do you think that students and faculty should be involved in the development of such a system, or should it be left to MIS professionals? Why or why not?

O'BRIEN AND GONSALVES

The law firm of O'Brien and Gonsalves, located in San Juan, Puerto Rico, has relied on PCs for several years. When they were first introduced the PCs were used primarily for word processing. Later on, software was added to keep track of client time charges and general accounting.

STAND-ALONE PCS

The PCs performed as stand-alone devices and were therefore unable to share data among computers or even to share programs. If a user needed to access data stored on another PC, or if a program used on another PC was needed, then a disk which included this data or program had to be taken from one machine and entered into the other.

Although this system had worked well and represented an enormous improvement over the labor-intensive methods used before word processing was introduced, there were many, including the staff of 14 lawyers, who expressed interest in expanding the system so that data and programs could be shared by all users. As one of the attorneys, Pedro Sanchez, explained, "It makes no sense not to be able to share memos. Right now I'm working on a case with two other lawyers in the firm, and it would save a lot of time if we could exchange documents and work on a brief without having to physically swap disks."

Another lawyer, Sally Friedman, had seen an interesting office mail system at a recent convention in Atlanta. The system allowed users to route **electronic mail** through PCs. In this process the writer entered the text into the PC using word processing software, and specified to whom the message was to be sent; the system then automatically stored the message and made it available to the designated recipient when that person requested a mail status report on the screen of his or her terminal.

The secretaries were also interested in an expanded system, capable of sharing files. Juanita Ortega explained that many times she prepared a document or letter not unlike one written by one of the other secretaries. If they could share their files it would reduce a lot of duplicated effort. Once the similar document is accessed and presented on the screen it could be modified. "A system like this could save me several hours of work every week."

Frank O'Brien, one of the senior partners in the firm, agreed that it was time to consider expanding the system, but was concerned that something different from what the firm had might prove too complicated to be really useful. He decided to bring in a consultant.

A LOCAL AREA NETWORK

Tom Williams of Information Design, a consulting firm that O'Brien and Gonsalves had used to set up its original word processing system, spent several hours at the firm talking with the staff and learning about their needs. At the end of the day he said that it sounded to him like the law firm needed to install the hardware and software necessary to link the computers in a **local area network**, which he called a **LAN**.

He explained that a LAN, in which several computers and other equipment are connected within a limited geographic area such as a department or building, could meet the company's need to share data as well as be used to support an electronic mail system.

"What type of hardware would we need?" asked O'Brien.

"The first step in selecting the hardware would be to determine how we should physically connect these machines. Two possibilities exist. We can have one computer act as a **controller**. It would be located at the center of our system, and linked directly to the other machines in the system. This configuration, or **topology**, would be called a **star topology**."

Williams went on to describe the second topology, which he referred to as a **ring topology**. "In this configuration, the computers are wired to a single cable which connects one computer to the next," Williams said. "It takes less cable to connect the equipment, but requires more sophisticated monitoring to make sure that only one user has access to the cable at a time. Otherwise collisions between users would occur."

"Would the cabling present a problem?" O'Brien asked. "What kind of cable are we talking about, anyway?"

"We've got several choices. We could use a shielded **twisted wire pair, coaxial cable**, or **fiber optic cable**."

O'Brien asked about the difference between them.

"First the price," Williams said. "The shielded twisted wire pair, not unlike the wires used to tie your telephones to the switchboard, would be the least expensive. Coaxial cable, or **coax** for short, like the cable used by cable TV companies to bring signals into your home, is more expensive. The most costly is fiber optic cable. But the advantage of moving up from twisted wire pair to the other choices is that data can be sent faster on the network, and the network can be expanded to carry more channels of information without the need to lay new cable. While we need to look into the choice more carefully, several of my clients in situations like yours have gone with coax.

"I would also recommend that we go with a token-passing ring network," continued Williams. In this type of design, a token is sent around the network. When a micro needs to send a message to another micro, it listens for the token. If it is available, the message is attached to the token and it then travels to its destination. Meanwhile, other micros needing to send messages cannot use the network until the token is free.

"In addition to the cabling required, each micro must have a network interface card inserted in one of its expansion slots so that it can participate in the network."

Williams went on to explain that files accessed by several different users would be stored centrally on a hard disk. Access and management of this data would be under the control of a computer called a **file server**. Another server to manage access to a letter quality printer or a laser printer should be included in the network. This would give all users the chance to share a high-quality printer.

"You should also be aware, Mr. O'Brien, that you will need software capable of functioning in a network environment. So we will have to look into new software, another expense that you must consider."

HIDDEN PROBLEMS

"Tom, I'm a little skeptical about this," Gonsalves said. "A firm with which we have collaborated in New York recently installed a network. One of the senior partners told me that they had plenty of problems. Just selecting the cables was difficult. Then the software they first chose wasn't sophisticated enough to do the job. They also had several different types of computers that needed to be interconnected, and that turned out to be a nightmare. They still don't have all the machines working on the network. And it turned out that training the employees to use the network was even more expensive than the network itself. Do you think we're biting off more than we can chew?"

QUESTIONS

1. Describe the current methods and procedures used in the O'Brien and Gonsalves law office.
2. What improvements could take place if the computers are connected and able to share files?
3. Define "local area network."
4. What are the choices for cabling the system that Williams proposes? Compare them in terms of advantages and characteristics.
5. Which topologies are under consideration? Compare them.
6. What is the function of a network interface card?
7. What does a file server do?
8. Can a laser printer be shared in the network?
9. Why do you think separate software is needed in a LAN?
10. Comment on the following statement. "A LAN is a very straightforward method for connecting computers and the process of developing the network need not involve the end-users, who are busy enough anyway."
11. Why is Gonsalves concerned? Do you agree with him?
12. What would be your next step.

WASTE INC.

"We've got to make sure that this network is flexible enough to add work stations at a minimum cost. What we want to avoid is a situation were it costs $3000 every time we need to add a new one to the system."

Fred Langley was expressing his concern to Alicia Young. Young, who works for the central data processing department at Waste Inc., is in the process of designing a local area network.

Waste Inc. is a rapidly growing company in the waste treatment and disposal business. They serve corporate and municipal customers and specialize in the cleanup of toxic waste sites and accidental chemical spills both on land and at sea.

Until now Waste relied on a central minicomputer and 53 microcomputers distributed throughout their office facilities, occupying three floors in an office building located in Chicago. The microcomputers were stand-alone devices and as a result they could not communicate with each other or with the mini. They were used for word processing, spreadsheet applications, and in about three cases supported small databases.

But with rapid growth, Waste was forced to choose between moving to a larger mini or installing a local area network to absorb some of the workload. When they were deciding which way to proceed, Young cited several advantages of a network. First, work stations could share data between micros, whereas now in order to share data, disks had to be passed between users. Second, several applications and parts of applications could be performed on the network and would reduce the load placed on the mini. Third, the network would provide micro users with access to mainframe data through a "gateway." Fourth, if the cabling system, used to connect the work stations, disk storage devices, and gateway in the network, was carefully chosen it would be relatively easy to expand the number of work stations in the network.

TOKEN RING TOPOLOGY

Several weeks ago Young announced that her department would recommend a token ringtopology. A **topology** is the physical description of how the workstations are arranged or laid out in a network. In a **token ring topology**, work stations are connected in a ring configuration.

Since there is one communication path in a ring and since it is likely that more than one work station may want to use this path to either communicate with other work stations, use peripheral devices such as the printer, or access the mini through the gateway, a ring network must have a mechanism for controlling this traffic and preventing collisions. This is done through the use of a **token** which is circulated through the network cabling. When a work station needs to communicate through the network it listens to see if the token is free. If it is, then the data, together with the destination's address, is attached to the token. The token then continues its journey until it finds its destination, at which place the data is delivered and the token resumes it's travel around the network until it is once again picked up by the next user. When a work station with data to send does not find the token free, it must wait until it is free before its data can be attached.

CABLING

Attention now turned to the cabling system required to connect the equipment in the network. And this is what Langley was concerned about. While he agreed with the choice of a ring topology, he felt strongly that a fiber optic cable should not be installed in the company and that a less expensive but less acceptable alternative be chosen.

"Why would you even consider twisted wire pair?" asked Langley.

"Several reasons. We already use it to connect our telephones, it isn't bulky like coaxial cable, and it costs only about 4 cents per foot."

"But I have heard that it's a bad choice because it is unshielded and as a result is susceptible to electromagnetic interference. In addition, twisted wire pair was designed to handle the low frequencies of telephones very well but is a poor way to connect high-data-rate signals, the kind that are produced by work stations. In fact you can pass at most 19.2 kilobits-per-second with a twisted pair. And this isn't very fast by todays standards where every computer connected to the network is capable of sending data at a rate of at least several hundred kilobits per second. In a ring topology, with several devices sending data, the network would not be able to keep up with the load."

"You're partially right," was Young's reply, "but recent developments with twisted wire pair have raised the transmission rate to 10 megabits-per-second, thereby providing a much higher throughput than was possible with conventional 19.2 kilobit-per-second systems. In fact high-quality twisted wire pair is being used with the IBM Cabling System.

"But this sytem is limited in its use to networks with only a few machines, and if we continue to grow the system won't keep up. We could be in trouble again."

"I don't see why we can't do it right and spend the money for a fiber optic cabling system, or at worst a coaxial system," was Langley's response. "These are the choices that make sense to me if you're going to span several floors in a building and plan to connect many machines. The coax can be relied on to send data at a rate between 300 and 500 megabits-per-second, while fiber optics is good for several thousand megabits. And these are the only alternatives that will allow us to mix voice, data, and even visuals.

"In fact, Alicia, I heard a consultant suggest that twisted wire pair would be phased out in the next 10 years and that coaxial cable would be phased out even before that. It seems to me the only logical choice, but an expensive one, would be fiber optic."

QUESTIONS

1. Why is Waste Inc. considering a LAN?
2. What can be done on a LAN that cannot be done using stand-alone microcomputers?
3. Describe a ring topology.
4. How are collisions prevented in a ring?
5. What is a twisted wire pair? What are its advantages when used in a network?
6. Compare coaxial cable and optic fiber cable.
7. Compare the transmission speeds of twisted wire pair, coaxial cable, and fiber optic cable.
8. Why is it important to make the right cabling decision before the network is installed?
9. What would be your next step if you had to make the decision?

OFFICE AUTOMATION AND WORD PROCESSING

Office automation refers to the use of information-processing and communication technologies for writing, collecting, storing, organizing, retrieving, and communicating office data. Some of the key technologies involved are word processing, electronic filing, electronic mail, and electronic conferencing. Increasingly, applications involving such technologies are being used in modern offices, with corresponding improvements in efficiency.

Two cases are presented in this section. In the first, a telephone switching systems manufacturer, Autoswitch, prepares documentation using word processing, and may move a step forward from that technology to desktop publishing. The second case, Olympic Homes, deals with a company that keeps overhead -- and consequently prices -- low in part through maintaining only a skeletal staff. However, customer service is also low; some possible remedies are presented.

AUTOSWITCH

Autoswitch, with offices and manufacturing facilities in a Chicago suburb, is a manufacturer of telephone switching systems used by telephone companies and large organizations.

An important part of the products they sell is the documentation which tells the user how to install, operate, and maintain the equipment. This documentation is prepared by the documentation department which includes a staff of 11 technical writers.

A **word processing** system, purchased five years ago, is used to prepare this documentation. The system includes eight stand-alone microcomputers and a popular, user-friendly software package.

The documentation process begins when the product development stage nears completion. At that time the technical writers start with their first draft. After several drafts and approval by management, the text together with rough sketches are sent to the graphics art department. There, graphs and illustrations are prepared by hand, and when completed the entire package is sent to typesetting, where professional-quality type with a resolution of 1200 dots per inch is produced. In the final step, the job is sent to an outside printing firm, copies are run on an offset press, and the finished product is bound.

DESKTOP PUBLISHING

The group manager of the documentation department, Roman Zar, prepared a proposal that would drastically alter the way work gets done. He proposes that Autoswitch purchase a new **desktop publishing system**.

"An important feature of a desktop publishing system," he explains in the memo, "is that this equipment will give us the ability to combine text, figures, graphics, and drawings and make adjustments on the screen. The technical writers in the group will be able to put the whole document together without the need for much involvement of the art department."

His boss, Hank Wade, manager of customer services, was skeptical. "Do we know anyone who has successfully gone in this direction?" Wade asked.

"Last week I visisted Wilson Automation," Zar said. "They recently bought a desktop publishing system, and the results have been dramatic. Wilson's system is probably close to what we will need. It includes a 32-bit processor, eight terminals, two 515-megabyte hard disk drives, three draft quality printers, and three laser printers.

Zar continued, "What impressed me about the system was the way in which they could integrate text, graphics, and drawings and create a library of art that all users could share. It seems that every time we develop a new manual, we start our illustration program from scratch. But with Wilson's system they enter the illustrations into the computer with a graphics interface device called a **mouse**, and then store the image. This then becomes their 'library art.' Then if that illustration, or one similar, is used in another manual, they don't redraw the image. It is retrieved and used as is, or modified using the mouse. Our current system of stand-alone micros here at Autoswitch makes sharing very difficult, but Wilson's system allows data to be shared by all of the users. This eliminates costly duplication of effort not only for illustrations but also for text.

"And the technical writers can see how the finished product will look," he continued. "It's all right there on their screen, text and graphics, exactly as it will appear in the finished document. When satisfied, a writer instructs the system to print a copy on the **laser printer**, which does top-quality work, and this becomes the master which is then sent to the print shop for offset duplication and binding."

IN DEFENSE OF THE OLD WAY

When the technicial writers at Autoswitch heard of the proposal, most were against it. Mary Phillips expressed her concern. "We're writers, not graphic artists. It's not our job to work with graphs and illustrations. We're not trained to do that!"

Ralph Kramden, another writer, was concerned about security. "If we can share each other's files, then what's to prevent someone from accidentally changing my work and ruining my schedule?"

Zar explained to Phillips that the technical writers could easily draw some of the simpler graphs and diagrams using the new equipment; the computer makes it relatively easy for non-commercial artists to do this. But more complex drawings could still be sent to the art department.

He explained to Kramden that the computer sytem would maintain file control over each individual's work. By using **passwords** and access codes, work could be protected so that it could be read and used in another application, but the original version could not be changed by the party who was borrowing it.

QUESTIONS

1. Describe the curent process used to produce finished documentation at Autoswitch.
2. What skills are needed by the technical writers at the present time?
3. What equipment or hardware is needed in a word processing system?
4. What software is needed in a word processing system?
5. How would Autoswitch use the proposed desktop publishing system? How would the job of the technical writers change?
6. Compare the word processing system currently in use with the proposed desktop publishing system. What is the difference?
7. Why is the new system's ability to share data between users an advantage?
8. Identify at least two major benefits from the new system.
9. What concerns have been raised about the new system?
10. Do you think system security would be a problem if Autoswitch moved to desktop publishing?
11. Should the technical writers be required to learn how to design charts, graphs, illustrations, and drawings?
12. If the new system is purchased, do you think an extensive training program should be planned? Explain.
13. If the president of the company suggested that it was wasteful to replace a computer system only five years old, how would you respond?
14. Would you recommend the purchase of the system? Or would you need more data -- if so, what type? -- before reaching a conclusion?

OLYMPIC HOMES

Olympic Homes, located in the Southwest, is a manufacturer of mobile and modular homes. Olympic competes in the low end of the market, with products in the $15,000 to $25,000 price range. Sales in the last three years have increased at a rate of about 20 percent annually, reaching $20 million last year.

In the annual report to stockholders, president Hal Thompson expressed the company's marketing philosophy in the following way: "Our customer is a first-time buyer who has been priced out of the conventional house market and who wants a no-frills home at an affordable price."

To keep prices affordable, Olympic has developed a modern and efficient manufacturing facility and a highly productive work force motivated by a participative management style and generous profit-sharing incentives.

A SKELETAL STAFF

But in addition to running an efficient manufacturing operation, Olympic also keeps overhead costs low. There are few management levels in the company and the number of people on the office staff is low.

One consequence of having a small staff is that customer service often suffers from inattention. In the last year, for example, dealers have been especially vocal about this issue. In one letter a Phoenix dealer wrote "We haven't received a reply from a letter sent two months ago! Please let us now if the awning option can be added to the Model 2200 series. If we don't receive a reply soon, we will lose another customer. Have others complained about your dealer service? Unless you do something about it, we will seriously consider terminating our relationship with Olympic."

And in another incident last year, both customers and dealers complained when questions about a leakage problem went unanswered until the factory recommended a solution some three months later.

The marketing department, which has the responsibility for responding to such inquiries, includes a staff of three individuals who act as the liaison among the factory, dealerships, and customers. But these three people are usually so overloaded with work that they are forced to put nonurgent inquiries aside, often permanently.

A PROPOSAL FREQUENTLY MADE

The director of marketing, Bruce Allard, has submitted, for the third time, a proposal recommending an increase in the staff. He argues that Olympic's success can be partially attributed to a tight supply in the market for modular homes. But he warns that as more manufacturers enter the market and capacity increases, so will competition. Without dealer and customer support, Olympic, he says, will eventually lose market share.

In his proposal Allard points out that only 25 percent of the inquiries from dealers are answered and less than five percent from customers. He wrote, "With a staff of three using conventional typewriters, it is impossible to keep up with the workload. We should be responding promptly to dealer questions about special options, about quality problems, about special state and federal laws that govern the transportation and use of these structures, about recommended repair procedures, and about replacement parts. I would also like our staff to have the capability to communicate directly with the customers who buy the homes. These customers should receive a follow-up letter after the purchase has been made, and we should respond directly to them when they write us about warranty coverage, repair problems, or the purchase of additional options. A satisified customer is our best advertisement.

"In addition to better servicing our customers," Allard's proposal went on, "I would like to have information that would be useful for marketing decisions. For example, it would be nice to have access to the data we already collect when a customer buys one of our homes. Last year we started to include a questionnare which the dealer has the customer fill out when the final paperwork is done. Customers answer questions relating to their age, education, income, proposed location of new home (private lot or mobile park), first or second home, how they learned about our product, other competitive units they considered, and so on. But when we receive these forms, they are placed in a storage box! I don't remember any time we actully looked at them. It would take too much time to make some generalizations about who our customers are and why they chose our product. But if we had a better filing system and a larger staff, perhaps we could gain some valuable insight that would help us understand our market better and guide us to more effective placement of our advertising and promotional dollars.

"With a larger staff I could have access to these data," the report continued, "The staff could summarize them in a table, and could prepare reports that show sales for our different product lines, warranty claims, and a host of other summary data that would help me make better marketing decisions.

"And I might add that I would like to use one of the additional staff to help produce brochures and product information bulletins that we send to our dealers. Now we send these jobs out to a professional printing shop, but the costs are high. We could produce these in-house at a significant cost savings."

QUESTIONS

1. Describe Olympic's business.
2. Why does Allard feel that more people are needed on his staff?
3. Do you think word processing would help the office become more productive? Why?
4. Give an example of how word processing could be used at Olympic.
5. Would you expect that there are several categories of letters that are sent to dealers and customers that are similar? If so, give an example, and explain how word processing could streamline the process of producing similar letters.
6. **Electronic filing** is the use of a computer to store and retrieve data. Would electronic filing be useful at Olympic? If so, give an example of data that might be filed and retrieved.
7. Is there any suggestion that electronic spreadsheets might be useful at Olympic? Explain.
8. Explain why desktop publishing might be useful. Why might it be beneficial to have this capability in-house?
9. If you were to use microcomputers for word processing, would you recommend that each staff member use a stand-alone micro -- one that cannot exchange data or programs with other microcomputers -- or would you recommend that the micros be linked together in a network so that data and programs could be shared? What would be the benefits from a network in this business environment?
10. What direction would you choose for Olympic -- more staff or office automation? What would be the next step you would take?

SECTION 10

SPREADSHEETS

An **electronic spreadsheet**, or **spreadsheet** for short, is a table with rows and columns into which data are entered. With spreadsheet software a user can enter data into a table format, manipulate the data, store the data, and print reports based on the data. The same thing can be done by hand, of course -- and was until electronic spreadsheets entered the picture in the 1970s -- but with a great deal more effort. The combination of spreadsheets and microcomputers places an important decision-support tool in the hands of modern management.

In this section cases are presented that both demonstrate the ways that spreadsheets are used and also give hands-on practice in working with spreadsheets yourself. The first case, Tampa Power Tool, describes how to capture budgets in a spreadsheet format. In the second case, budgeting at the the Centurion Palace Hotel is described, with another chance to set up several spreadsheets yourself. At Pix Studios, the motion picture producers of the third case, "what if" questions are posed using a spreadsheet concerning the complexities of movie-making; here too you can participate. In the final case, Nobo Appliance, a wholesale distributor, faces a specific problem of stocking a very expensive item that might not have been solved at all without the use of a spreadsheet; hands-on practice is provided here as well.

TAMPA POWER TOOL

Tampa Power Tool, a manufacturer of tools for the home handyman, has been manufacturing electric workshop tools for more than 30 years. Their electric drills, saber saws, circular saws, and jig saws are sold in many hardware and discount stores. One year ago Tampa enlarged their product line and introduced electrical kitchen appliances including countertop ovens, toaster ovens, toasters, and blenders.

Every quarter at Tampa Power Tool a manufacturing budget is prepared. The purpose of this budgeting process is to estimate sales figures and then determine the financial, labor, and equipment resources necessary to support this level of output. During this year's budgeting session one of the manufacturing managers, Andy Waselik, suggested to the vice-president of manufacturing, Del King, that the budgets for the workshop and home applicance lines be separated. He argued that separate facilities are used to make these products, and by separating them in the budget they would have more useful data for planning and control of operations.

The current budget includes the following categories:

> SALES
> DIRECT LABOR COST
> RAW MATERIAL COST
> MACHINE COST
> UTILITY COSTS
> TRANSPORTATION COSTS
> DEPRECIATION
> STAFF SALARIES
> RENT
> OFFICE EXPENSES
> OTHER EXPENSES
> OPERATING PROFIT

Wasilik suggested that three budget worksheets be prepared. The first would summarize the costs for the workshop line, the second would summarize the costs for the appliance line, and the third, an aggregate budget, would include a total of costs from both lines.

"I've broken down the budget for next quarter," Waselik said, "and here is what it would look like for the workshop line."

SALES	$500(000,000)

DIRECT LABOR COST	80
RAW MATERIAL COST	135
MACHINE COST	15
UTILITY COST	10
TRANSPORTATION COST	14
DEPRECIATION	20
STAFF SALARIES	35
RENT	50
OFFICE EXPENSE	12
OTHER EXPENSES	9
TOTAL COSTS	380
OPERATING PROFIT	120

Wasilik then showed what the budget would look like for the appliance line.

SALES	$30(000,000)

DIRECT LABOR COST	5
RAW MATERIAL COST	5
MACHINE COST	2
UTILITY COST	1
TRANSPORTATION COST	3
DEPRECIATION	2
STAFF SALARIES	2
RENT	5
OFFICE EXPENSE	1
OTHER EXPENSES	1
TOTAL COSTS	27
OPERATING PROFIT	3

King liked the idea. "Andy, do you think we could get these budgets on the computer? If we could, they would be a lot easier to work with, and if they were easily accessible it might give us a better chance to hit our targets.

QUESTIONS

1. Can these budgets be entered into a spreadsheet? Why?
2. Design a spreadsheet in such a way that it has three sections that will include the three complete budgets. In the top section will be the budget for the workshop tool product line. Skip several lines and place the kitchen appliance budget in the next section, then skip several more lines and design a budget which sums the two above it.
3. Enter the data in your spreadsheet, and check to see that it calculates operating profit correctly.
4. Suppose direct labor costs increased in the workshop product line from 80 to 110. Enter this change in the spreadsheet and observe the change on operating profit. Have the direct cost and operating profit figures for the combined budget changed?
5. Revise your spreadsheet so that a new column is entered next to the column in which cost estimates will be entered. This new column will include actual expenses and can be used to compare actual and budgeted figures.
6. Return to question 5, and enter another column which will compute the amount by which the actual costs exceeded the budgeted costs.
7. Return to question 5, and enter the following actual costs into your spreadsheet.

	WORKSHOP	KITCHEN
SALES	425	25
DIRECT LABOR COST	95	4
RAW MATERIAL COST	120	7
MACHINE	12	2
UTILITY COST	11	1
TRANSPORTATION COST	15	2
DEPRECIATION	20	1
STAFF SALARIES	34	4
RENT	50	3
OFFICE EXPENSE	13	2
OTHER EXPENSE	11	2

CENTURION PALACE HOTEL

The Centurion Palace Hotel is a large urban hotel built in 1928 and renovated several times since. Guests at the hotel are offered a full range of services including three restaurants, a coffee shop, a health club, and retail stores. Revenues last year were over $16 million, with a profit after taxes of $1 million.

Every six months management prepares a cash budget for the following six-month period. At the present time the budget is being prepared for January through June. The purpose of this budget is to determine the cash requirements of the hotel over this period. Management can determine from the budget, for example, when the peak demands for cash will occur. With this information they may be able to delay some capital expenditures, if necessary, or plan on delaying payment for purchases. But if these steps are still not enough to ensure that necessary payments can be made, then the hotel must plan for either short- or long-term borrowing.

The budget is also used to identify those periods in which the cash flow is positive; during those periods plans are made to invest the funds in marketable securities and receive interest. The result would be a transfer of funds from cash in one month to marketable securities in another month and then back to cash in a following month.

SALES FORECAST

The budget begins with a forecast of revenues. Several sources of revenues are considered in the forecast. First, occupancy rates are estimated, and then estimates are made for each of the hotel's other services, including restaurants, coffee shop, and health club. The importance of this forecast has always been emphasized. It becomes the basis for all of the other estimates, and errors in the sales forecast will bias the entire projection.

CASH RECEIPTS

Once the sales forecast has been completed, the next step is to determine cash receipts. When a sale is made for cash, cash is received immediately. But most of the sales made at the hotel are credit sales and cash is not received until some time after the sale has been made. The hotel's experience has been that approximately

10 percent of their sales are cash sales; 90 percent of the credit sales are received one month from the date of the sale; 10 percent of the credit sales are received two months from the date of the sale; and the hotel suffers no bad debts.

For the coming period from November to June the sales forecast has been estimated.

MONTH	FORECAST
NOVEMBER	$300
DECEMBER	350
JANUARY	250
FEBRUARY	200
MARCH	250
APRIL	300
MAY	350
JUNE	380

For November, we can see that sales are $300. Cash receipts for this month will be $30, while $270 will be credit sales. Ninety percent of the credit sales, or $243, will be collected in December, and ten percent, or $27, in January.

EXPENSES

The next step in the budgeting process involves the forecast of cash disbursements. In this step the department managers must submit an estimate of the purchases they expect to make over this period and the wages they expect to pay.

Most purchases are made on a credit basis, and payment is not required until one month after the purchase is made. Wages, on the other hand, must be paid in the month incurred.

In the chart shown next, the estimates are given for purchases and wages. In addition, "other" expenses are included for each month.

MONTH	PURCHASES	WAGES	OTHER
DECEMBER	$100		
JANUARY	80	80	50
FEBRUARY	100	80	50
MARCH	120	90	50

MONTH	PURCHASES	WAGES	OTHER
APRIL	140	90	50
MAY	150	95	50
JUNE	150	100	50

For January, we can see that purchases will be $80 but cash payment for purchases will be $100, since December's purchases are due and paid in January. In addition, wages paid in January are $80 and other expenses are $50. Total cash expenses in January are therefore $100 + $80 + $50 = $230.

In addition to cash expenses, capital expenditures must also be taken into consideration. Because capital expenditures are considered far in advance, they usually are predictable for the short-term budget. The Centurion Palace Hotel has scheduled a renovation project, the costs of which will be $150 in February and $50 in March.

Since dividend payments to the hotel's stockholders have been stable and are not expected to change, the budget will include $20 of dividend payments in April.

Estimation for federal income taxes is also an important category in the budget. These estimates are based on projected earnings of the corporation for the period covered by the budget. Estimated taxes for the Centurion Palace are $30 in January and $30 in June.

ASSIGNMENT

1. Using spreadsheet software, construct a schedule of sales receipts for the period November through June. In this schedule include the following categories:

> Total sales
> Credit sales
> Collections -- one month
> Collections -- two months
> Total collections
> Cash sales
> Total sales receipts

Several entries will be missing for the months of November and December, but this budget is for the period January to June and the missing entries will not affect the way in which the budget will be used.

2. Skip several lines on your spreadsheet and begin to develop a schedule of expenses. In this schedule include the following categories:

> Purchases
> Cash payment for purchases
> Wages paid
> Other expenses
> Total cash expenses

3. Skip several lines in your spreadsheet and develop a cash disbursement schedule that includes the following categories:

> Total cash expenses (see above)
> Capital expenditures
> Dividend payments
> Income taxes
> Total cash disbursements

4. Skip several lines on your spreadsheet and develop a net cash-flow schedule. In this schedule, total cash disbursements are subtracted from total cash receipts, to obtain net cash flow. Next, the net cash flow for the month is added to the beginning cash for the month (this is the same as the ending cash flow for the previous month) to obtain an ending cash flow for the current month. In January, assume that the beginning cash is $100. Include the following categories:

> Total cash receipts (see above)
> Total cash disbursements (see above)
> Net cash flow
> Beginning cash without financing
> Ending cash without financing

5. Cash budgets are merely estimates. The actual cash flow that eventually occurs will be either greater or less than the estimates. In the face of this uncertainty it only seems reasonable to prepare several budgets, each representing possible scenarios. The one that was just constructed represents the most likely outcome for the hotel. But the season could be either very good or very bad. Under each of these circumstances, what would be the effect on the net cash flow? To answer this question, prepare two additional spreadsheets. Sales estimates for each possibility are given below. Enter the new data, and obtain a printout of each budget.

SALES ESTIMATES UNDER OPTIMISTIC CONDITIONS

NOVEMBER	$325
DECEMBER	365
JANUARY	275
FEBRUARY	200
MARCH	260
APRIL	330
MAY	375
JUNE	425

SALES ESTIMATES UNDER PESSIMISTIC CONDITIONS

NOVEMBER	$250
DECEMBER	325
JANUARY	240
FEBRUARY	175
MARCH	240
APRIL	275
MAY	325
JUNE	350

PIX STUDIOS

The meeting was filled with tension. Ted Thorner was in the process of presenting the financial summary from the most recent Pix release.

"We've got nothing short of another disaster on our hands," Thorner said. "The reviews stink, the box office sales are far short of what we needed, and ticket sales are already dwindling."

The movie that Thorner was referring to was originally budgeted for $28 million. It finally came in at a cost of $53 million, and if it lost only $15 million, Pix would be lucky.

Pix is a nationally recognized producer of movies, episodes in television series, and made-for-TV movies. While the bulk of profits in the past came from box office sales and network TV sales, profits now mainly come from the sale of video cassettes of Pix films and from deals with pay-cable companies.

INDUSTRY TREND

Like most other film producers, Pix was undergoing difficult times. The costs to produce a motion picture or television episode had increased greatly in recent years. Although box office revenue had also increased, the higher revenues did not offset the higher costs. Costs, esecially such "above-the-line" costs as the salaries demanded by top-name actors and producers, were astronomical. One Pix star was demanding $16 million to do a sequel to a profitable movie.

According to industry sources, the average cost to make a movie has risen from about $2 million in 1975, to $8 million in 1980, and to $18 million in 1987. And this doesn't include overhead and marketing costs, which today can amount to more than another $8 million. Deciding to produce a movie is a $26 million decision!

At the meeting Thorner said that the video-cassette and pay-TV deals could no longer be relied upon to pull Pix out of movies that lost money. "We'll have to carefully examine the projected costs and revenues with every movie project before we begin, and the proposal we have to consider today is a good place to start. I don't think I have to tell you that another disaster like the one we have on our hands right now could put an end to our operation."

NEW PROJECT

Thorner was referring to a proposal for a new action-packed military adventure set in troubled Central America. Thorner was determined to keep costs for this film low.

"Let's look at above-the-line costs first," he said. The above-the-line costs in the movie industry are related to the talent and include money spent for story rights, script, director, producer, and actors.

The cost for the producer would be $795,986; actors would cost $1,913,532; story rights would be $74,665; script development would be $313,085; and the cost for the director would be $427,972. These costs do not include the salaries paid to key personnel, but do include allowances for secretaries and assistants to these individuals.

Below-the-line costs include production and post-production costs. Included in this project are $2,000,000 for set design and development; $890,000 for transportation; $327, 984 for wardrobe; $227,750 for "extras;" $197,341 for props; $327,000 for music; $146,321 for sound; $1,393,000 for film processing and editing; and $4,262,137 for special effects.

None of these costs include an allocation for the overhead costs, which pay for the use of studio departments such as the carpentry and paint shops, for shooting on sound stages, and for the salaries of studio executives. Usually overhead represents 15 percent of the combined talent and production costs.

Thorner walked to the blackboard and began writing. "Sales at the box office for this project should be about $12 million," he said as he wrote, "and we receive 45 percent of this gross. We can also sell about 150,000 video cassettes at a retail price of $89.95, and our wholesale net will be $56. Expenses would include royalties and the cost of physically producing the cassettes, and would total about $9 per cassette.

"We should be able to strike a deal with a pay-cable provider and generate another $4 million in revenue, and this figure will probably include the small amount we receive from showings on airplanes and independent television stations."

BETTER FINANCIAL ANALYSIS NEEDED

When Thorner finished, the group began to discuss the project from a marketing point of view, and after 30 minutes, Louise Jensen interrupted. "If we're so concerned about the profitability of these projects," she said, "why aren't we spending more time examining the costs and revenues? Since these projects are so risky, don't you think we should see what the consequences are if the film flops and we receive only a fraction of what we expected?"

"You're right, Louise," Thorner replied. "It's late to get started on this today, but do you think you could work up some figures for us and we'll meet again tommorrow at ten?"

QUESTIONS

1. Prepare a spreadsheet that includes the data initially presented by Thorner. Your spreadsheet should list the above-the-line costs, below-the-line costs, overhead, and profit.
2. Identify the sources of risk in this project.
3. **Sensitivity analysis** helps the decision-maker explore the consequence of **risk**. In this analysis certain data are changed to reflect the possibilty that the outcome in some categories might be better or worse than expected. Explain how sensitivity analysis would be useful in this situation.
4. What if box office sales totalled only $10 million, only 60,000 video cassettes were sold, and the deal with cable TV produced only $3 million? What impact would this have on project profitability?
5. Every movie producer hopes for a blockbuster. Suppose box office sales zoomed to $20 million, 200,000 cassettes were sold, and cable TV paid $7 million for the rights to show the film. How would profitability be affected?

NOBO APPLIANCE

Nobo Appliance is a wholesale distributor of household appliances, stereos, and TV sets. Nobo's customers include 450 retail stores within a 150-mile radius of its warehouse.

Nobo orders in large quantities from manufacturers or importers, and then sells to customers whose retail sales volume is too low to warrant direct purchasing from these sources.

One of the partners, Bill Oremland, was puzzling over a problem that he hadn't encountered before. New large-screen television sets were selling extremely well, but their high cost -- higher than any other item he carried, and many with retail price tags of over $3000 -- prevented him from ordering large quantities at a time. Yet he knew if he didn't have stock to meet demand, retailers would order from one of the other distributors in the area.

Oremland described his concern to his business parter, Peter Revere.

"Peter, there just doesn't seem to be an obvious answer." Oremland was pointing to a sales forecast for the wide-screen units. "We can't order every few weeks because the cost is simply too high. It must cost us about $200 -- in ordering and paperwork costs -- to bring in a shipment regardless of how many units we order. So to save us from running up a huge ordering tab, we shouldn't order more than once every few months.

"But on the other hand," Oremland continued, "if we order infrequently these units will cost us quite a bit to store in our warehouse. They're big and we have to keep special insurance on them. I figure it will cost us about $30 to keep a unit from one month to the next.

"My instinct says we should place an order every two months. What do you think, Peter?"

Revere looked at the sales forecast but concluded that orders should be placed every month because carrying costs are so high.

"The order costs are peanuts compared to our other costs," Revere said. "I don't think we should even consider order costs. And besides, we need that tight control over ordering to make sure we have enough in stock to meet demand. Every time we can't ship a large-screen unit because we're out of stock we lose about $100 in profit. We need to order at least once every month!"

Joe Forgione, the accounting manager, had sat down at the table several minutes earlier and had been listening to Oremland describe his dilemma. He had a suggestion. "I wonder if we could build a spreadsheet model of this problem that would take into consideration all of these costs, and then let us play around with different ordering strategies. It might help us to understand the problem better."

A week later Forgione brought some computer output to Oremland and Revere. "What I've got is a spreadsheet **template** that lets you try different ordering strategies," Forgione said. "After you move the cursor to the appropriate cell under the column labeled `order' and enter an order amount, it will tell you what the sum is of the three major costs you two were talking about last week. It computes the ordering costs for each order, the carrying costs to carry month-end inventory over into the next month, and it also computes an out-of-stock penalty if you run out of stock."

The three of them returned to Forgione's office to take a look at the spreadsheet model (Figure 1). Oremland entered the data corresponding to orders every other month. The software quickly computed the total cost of $17,177. Then Revere tried entering just two orders, one in January and the other in July. Costs increased to $21,880.

"Joe, the fixed order costs, inventory carry costs, and out-of-stock penalties are just estimates," Oremland commented. "Could we try some other estimates to see what impact they would have on total costs?"

"All you have to do," Forgione said, "is to move the cursor to cell E4 and enter the new fixed-order-cost estimate, move the cursor to cell G5 and enter the new carrying cost estimate, and then move the cursor to cell E7 and enter the new out-of-stock penalty.

"Before we bring this disk back to our micro and try some other alternatives, could you explain what the column headings mean?" Oremland asked.

Forgione explained the following headings.

MONTH
This column includes the month in the planning period.

FORECAST
Entered in this column is the forecast over the planning period. If it is necessary to try a new forecast to determine how this change in demand would affect inventory strategy, the new forecast numbers would be entered into these cells and the new data would automatically initiate a recalculation of all costs.

OPENING BALANCE
This column usually includes the opening balance that will be available at the start of the new month. Notice that it is the same as the end-of-month balance for the previous month.

ORDER
This is the column into which the user enters the
orders that will be placed over the planning
horizon. But orders placed here won't be
available for sale until just after the beginning
of the next month.

ORDER COST
The computer automatically charges a fixed cost
for every order placed. The dollar amount appears
in this column.

ENDING BALANCE
This figure is automatically computed and
represents the ending balance: opening balance +
order arrivals - forecast demand.

CARRYING COST
The numbers in this column represent the cost to
carry inventory from one month into the next. It
is automatically computed by the software.

OUT-OF-STOCK PENALTY
The cost charged when there is not enough stock to
meet demand. It generally includes lost profit
and may even include future lost profits because
customers may be permanently lost to the
competition.

TOTAL ORDER + CARRYING + PENALTY COSTS
This is the total of all three costs for each
month.

QUESTIONS

1. Describe the problem which Nobo must solve.
2. Why is it difficult, in this situation, to reach a decision without the help of a
   computer?

3. How would you classify a computer system that helped Oremland make this decision -- a transaction system or a Management Information System?
4. In Forgione's model what is meant by the opening balance?
5. Where are the data for orders entered into the model?
6. How are order costs computed?
7. How is ending balance computed?
8. What are carrying costs? How are they computed?
9. Why and when are out-of-stock penalties incurred?
10. If you have access to the model on a computer, enter the data shown in Figure 1 and verify the result.
11. Make the following changes and run the model.
    Fixed order charges: $500
    Cost to carry inventory: $20
    Out-of-stock penalty: $100
12. Return to original spreadsheet template and try other ordering strategies. Can you find an ordering strategy with lower costs than Oremland or Revere found?

SECTION 11

TRANSACTION SYSTEMS

Transaction systems are computer systems used to process the routine day-to-day information flows in an organization. Transaction systems keep records of routine business activities, follow standard operating procedures, do not require complex decisionmaking, depend on accurate and detailed data, and must be able to process large volumes of these data in short periods of time.

The "workhorses" of most centralized computer centers, transaction systems are vital to modern organizations. Some businesses, such as large airlines and banks, could not exist without them. Not only do transaction systems support the actual work that an organization does, but they serve as a foundation upon which Management Information Systems and Decision Support Systems can build to help guide the direction of the organization.

Cases are presented in this section that not only show what transaction systems are and how they work but provide practice in using them. Pacific North Press, a publishing house, offers a very high level of customer service thanks in part to its transaction systems. The transaction system characteristics described in this case include batch versus on-line transaction processing, voice input, and the use of laptop computers for remote data entry by the sales staff.

The next case concerns Thomas Greenhouses Inc, and is split into three parts. A tiny business that blossomed into a major undertaking, Thomas Greeenhouses hires a consultant to help bring the firm back to financial health. The details of the computer-based accounting information system suggested by the consultants are given, and with the help of the accompanying software and step-by-step instructions, you will have the chance to build and use the accounting system.

PACIFIC NORTH PRESS

Pacific North Press has published thousands of titles since it began operations in 1948. Just in the last five years, 22 titles have been on the national best-seller list for at least one week, several of them in first place.

Pacific North publishes over 1600 fiction and nonfiction titles in hard cover and paperback, including books for young readers. In addition they sell computer software and books on tape.

Although it is certainly important for Pacific to publish books written by the most talented writers and interesting people around, it is also vital that behind-the-scenes business operations function smoothly and efficiently.

CUSTOMER SERVICE

"Customer service is very important to us," said John Walters, Pacific's vice-president of administration. "This April we will ship a record ten million books to stores across the United States and Canada to fulfill some one hundred thousand separate orders for new titles and titles which we previously introduced, called backlist titles. A wholesaler in Los Angeles may order different quantities of each of a hundred titles, while a bookseller in Toronto may order just two dozen copies of our number-one best seller. And it is our policy to get both accounts their exact orders with the fastest turnaround that is possible."

To provide its customers with this level of service, Pacific North relies heavily on computers. Walters explained that the company has to make sure that every bookstore in town receives a new book on the same day it is released. This means not only getting it to over one hundred thousand retailers simultaneously, but making sure that some three hundred wholesalers have it in time to distribute to their customers on the same day.

Until eight years ago Pacific did all its data processing through a time-sharing agreement with another publisher. That computer system used **batch processing** methods, and as a result sales order processing was slow. At that time Pacific North decided to begin to build a system that could handle **on-line processing** to provide immediate access to a central database of inventory and orders.

Today, the company has two DEC superminicomputers, and a host of micros tied together in a network. One supermini is located in the New York office and handles Pacific's financial applications. Another in Chicago handles inventory, sales order entry, and returns. Both are tied together through a microwave network.

SALES ORDER ENTRY AND INVENTORY CONTROL

Carlos Feliciano, director of planning, explained the Chicago operation. "We receive orders through the mail, by telephone, and by magnetic tape. The tape system was installed two years ago and is working out very well. By using an agreed-upon industry format that was developed by booksellers, our customers can record their orders on magnetic tape, send us the tape, and then we can enter the order directly into our computer system.

"We also use a **voice output** system developed by a major communications company that allows our salespeople in the field to enter their customer orders directly into the computer from any pushbutton telephone," Feliciano continued. "With this system the salesperson dials the computer center in Chicago, and when the line is answered a computer simulated voice requests several pieces of data to be entered with the pushbuttons of the telephone. First the voice requests requests the salesperson's ID, and then it pauses for the data entry. Next the voice requests the customer's ID. Then it requests the product ID for the product ordered, it pauses for a response, and then requests the number ordered. After a pause it asks for the next product ID number, and continues to collect order data in this way until the user presses the "*" button to terminate the order.

"As soon as an order is entered," Feliciano went on, "the system automatically performs a credit check on the account and an inventory check to see if the titles are in stock. If a title is not in stock it is automatically backordered. When new titles arrive in the warehouse from the printer and after the data concerning these new arrivals are entered into a terminal, the system automatically reviews the backorder list to determine if any of the backordered titles are now in stock. If they are in stock, then shipping can be initiated.

"Even if the customer credit check reveals a problem," Feliciano explained, "the computer places those orders in a queue and sends them to our credit department in a batch, every hour. Credit analysts review the reports and in most cases approve the order the same day."

Once the order is approved, the picking documents are printed in the warehouse, and after the warehouse personnel assemble and package it, they confirm its shipment through an entry into their terminals. At that time inventory records are updated to reflect the depletions made, and the Chicago system communicates with the New York system so that the appropriate accounting records can be updated and an invoice mailed to the customer.

"All of these steps use the on-line facilities of the computer system, so the turnaround from the receipt of the order to the shipment of the order is very fast," Feliciano said.

IMPROVED DATA ENTRY

Although the telephone order-entry system has worked well, Feliciano feels that it has two shortcomings. First, it takes the salesperson a long time to enter the order. Second, it limits the salesperson's access to central data. Feliciano would like the salesperson to be able to access inventory and backorder data so that the customer can learn immediately if a title is in stock and when it can be shipped. Feliciano has proposed that Pacific purchase small laptop computers for their sales staff and develop the software to support these functions. With specially designed screens for these units, orders and inquiries would be easier to enter, and once entered, the data could be sent in the batch mode from the customer's location to the computer over the telephone network.

QUESTIONS

1. Describe the business that Pacific North is in.
2. Why are efficient order processing and inventory control systems necessary?
3. A **transaction system** is described as a system that (1) helps an organization carry out its routine day-to-day business efficiently; (2) is operated by clerks or other individuals who need little training in how to use the system and use it not as a general tool but in specific, well-defined, and repetitive ways; (3) does not require the user to make any decisions of major consequence to the firm; (4) can handle a high volume of detailed data generated by the daily activities of the business; and (5) is in constant use. Comparing each of the five points mentioned above with the case, determine if the sales order entry and inventory control systems can be classified as a transaction system.
4. Describe the flow of data from order entry through inventory update and billing.
5. Why would a strictly batch processing transaction system for Pacific North be inadequate?
6. How would you describe the business objectives of this system?
7. Describe the difference between on-line and batch processing. Give an example of each from the case.
8. What is source data automation? How is this used at Pacific North?
9. Give an example of data input to the system.
10. Give an example of data output.

11. Compare the current method of data entry by pushbutton telephone to the proposed system which would use laptop units. Which would you recommend? Why?
12. What type of management information do you think might be obtained from the data stored in this system?

THOMAS GREENHOUSES INC.
(PART ONE)

In 1975 Art Thomas opened a greenhouse business on his front lawn. First-year sales were a surprising $20,000. Now Thomas Greenhouses Inc. is one of the largest growers in the Northeast. The product line includes over 100 varieties of houseplants, over 200 varieties of seedlings for spring plantings, and over 1250 varieties of trees and shrubs. In addition, Thomas also carries a complete line of garden tools and supplies ranging from insecticides to rototillers.

Art Thomas received his degree in botany, and his research specialty in school had been the study of tuberous begonias. After school he continued to work in this area, and it is for begonias that Thomas Greenhouses is best known. On several occasions Thomas has won prizes for his begonias, and this recognition has helped him land several top accounts from sports complexes and shopping malls that are steady, large-volume users of plants, trees, shrubs, and supplies.

As the company grew, so, of course, did its problems. In recent years seasonal borrowing costs have mushroomed, and profits as a percent of sales have been in decline. To reverse this problem, Thomas hired a consulting firm to analyze the system and procedures used by his company and to recommend any changes that might help return it to a more profitable position.

The consulting firm found a company that was ruled by the iron hand of its founder. Systems put into place a decade or more ago remained unchanged, and few suggestions from employees for improvements met with a positive reception. In particular, the consultants felt that the accounting system was inadequate. Records were seldom accurate and there seemed to be little emphasis on financial controls. Never, for example, had the company developed a budget, and never had the company monitored its financial performance over time.

The current accounting system uses the "two-write" system. In this system an oversized notebook holds both checks and record sheets. These record sheets are called "ledger sheets." When a check is written, the amount is automatically copied in carbon on the ledger sheet under the cash column. In addition, a second entry is made by the accounting clerk under the appropriate expense column on the ledger sheet. At the end of the month these expense categories are totaled and summarized, and at the end of each year both profit and loss statements (Figure 1) and balance sheets (Figure 2) are prepared.

Profit and Loss Statement
Thomas Greenhouses, Inc.
December 31, 1987

Sales(000)		11,200
Cost of Goods Sold		
Beginning Inventory	2,100	
Purchases	4,500	
Less Ending Inventory	2,000	4,600
Gross Profit		6,600
Sales and Administrative		2,500
Wages		2,000
Depreciation		1,000
Taxes		500
Net Profit		600

Figure 1. Profit and loss statement for Thomas Greenhouse, Inc.

Balance Sheet
Thomas Greenhouse, Inc.
December 31, 1987

Current Assets		Current Liabilities	
Cash(000)	300	Accounts Payable	1,000
Accounts Receiable	500		
Inventories	2,000		
Fixed Assets		Stockholders Equity	
Plant and Equipment	13,700	Capital	6,000
		Retained Earnings	9,500
Total Assets	16,500	Total Liabilities	16,500

Figure 2. Balance Sheet for Thomas Greenhouse, Inc

It was not easy for Thomas to bring in consultants to help him. To make matters worse, the consultants felt that Thomas desperately needed a computer accounting system. When Thomas read their report, he remembered a conversation with one of his friends at last year's flower show in Philadelphia. His friend had installed a computerized accounting system only to find that the computer had cost him more money than it had saved. His friend's accounting staff had gone from one full-time and one part-time employee to three full-time people!

Thomas, somewhat confused, packed the report into his briefcase and prepared to leave for the weekend. Perhaps, he thought, he might come up with the answer before Monday.

QUESTIONS

Assume that you are one of the consultants hired by Art Thomas. Answer the following questions.

1. Explain the purpose of an accounting information system.
2. What benefits would you expect from an improved accounting information system?
3. Is an accounting information system a transaction system or a Management Information System?
4. As a company grows, how would you expect its information system needs to change?
5. Do you think a computer system can help return a troubled company to financial health?
6. Describe the input requirements of an accounting information system.
7. Describe the output requirements of an accounting information system.
8. What is a profit and loss statement? Describe the difference between gross and net profit.
9. What is a balance sheet? Describe the difference between assets and liabilities.
10. How should the organization of a project such as this take shape? Should all the details be left to the consultants, or do you think management and end-users should be involved in project development?
11. Identify what you think the major pitfalls might be of a project such as this.

THOMAS GREENHOUSES INC. (PART TWO)

NOTE: This case involves some very basic priciples usually covered in an introductory course in accounting. While the case does introduce and illustrate these principles on a very elementary level, some students may find it necessary to review other sources. The primary objective of the case, however, is not to introduce accounting concepts but to give the reader practical exposure to a very realistic transaction processing system.

Your instructor has a copy of the accounting software discussed in this case. You are free to make copies of it for use on your own computer or in your schol's lab. You will need it to follow the example and complete the assignments in this and the following case.

ABC Consulting, hired to bring Thomas Greenhouses back to financial health, suggested a computer-based accounting information system. The software ABC recommends is a general-purpose accounting system used by many of their clients. But before the system can be implemented, Thomas Greenhouses must study the way in which the new system will be used. First Thomas must review the **chart of accounts** currently in use. Then Thomas must determine if this set of accounts is capable of providing them with the information necessary to maintain financial control of the company. If the current chart of accounts is inadequate, then a new chart of accounts must be designed

CURRENT CHART OF ACCOUNTS

Thomas Greenhouses now uses a simple chart of accounts.

ACCOUNT
****
SALES
GENERAL & ADMINISTRATIVE EXPENSE
WAGES (EXPENSE)
DEPRECIATION EXPENSE
PLANT & EQUIPMENT
CASH
INVENTORY

PURCHASES (EXPENSE)
COST OF GOODS SOLD
ACCOUNTS RECEIVABLE
ACCOUNTS PAYABLE
RETAINED EARNINGS
CAPITAL
TAXES PAID

Because Thomas Greenhouses has little experience with sophisticated accounting systems, ABC Consulting has suggested that their present accounting system be used as the basis for a prototype of the new system. If Thomas finds this prototype satisfactory, then the system will be expanded.

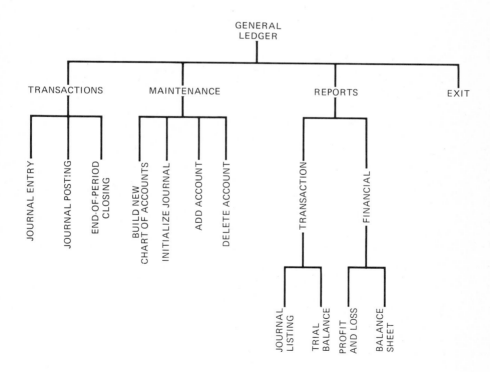

Figure 1. The structure of the general ledger system.

THE ACCOUNTING SYSTEM

The accounting software to be used by Thomas (see the note at the beginning of this case) can be described as a menu-driven system that can be be tailored to each user's needs. The system can accomodate up to 99 accounts, provides **audit trails** for journal entries, and will print financial statements. In many ways this software is similar to the products sold commercially and will give you the opportunity to experience how transaction applications are designed and used.

The menus in the system provide a guided path through which the user can enter data, obtain responses to queries, and print financial reports. The structure of this menu-driven system is shown in Figure 1.

To use the software which accompanies this case you will need:
- o An IBM PC or compatable
- o A copy of BASICA or GW-BASIC
- o A formatted blank disk for your data

To load the software follow these steps:
- o Boot your computer
- o Remove the disk used to boot the system
- o Enter a Basic disk in drive A and,
  depending upon the version of basic, enter
      A> BASIC
- o When the rectangular cursor appears
  remove the BASIC disk from drive A and
  insert the program disk in drive A. Then
  enter
      RUN "GL"
- o The first screen of the general ledger
  package will soon come into view.
- o Now remove the program disk from drive A
  and insert your data disk in drive A.
- o After pressing the return key to move from
  the first to the second screen, you will
  enter today's date, and the system will
  be ready to be used.

ESTABLISHING A CHART OF ACCOUNTS

The first step in building a new system requires the user to identify the chart of accounts to be used in the general ledger. Once identified, the software can be customized to include these accounts. Since Thomas will first build a prototype, the simple chart of accounts currently in use will be the basis for the new system.

From the main menu of the accompanying software, select "2," which represents "maintenance." This will take you to the maintenance menu, and from this menu you should select "1," which represents "build new chart of accounts."

At this point you will enter the account numbers and names. No balances for these accounts are entered now. This will be left to a later step.

The account number for a specific account must fall within the appropriate ranges shown below. For example, a sales account must be numbered from 1 to 5, or the wages account must have number between 6 and 49.

ACCOUNT RANGE	ACCOUNT
01 - 05	SALES
06 - 49	EXPENSES
50 - 57	CURRENT ASSETS
58 - 64	OTHER ASSETS
65 - 72	CURRENT LIABILITIES
73 - 79	OTHER LIABILITIES
80 - 89	CAPITAL
99	RETAINED EARNINGS

Note that the retained earnings account must be account 99. Also note that account names must be limited to no more than 13 characters, therefore some account names must be abbreviated. For example, 'cost of goods sold' could be abbreviated to 'CGS'.

TRIAL BALANCE

Once the chart of accounts has been established, return to the main menu and select the "report" option. This will bring you to the report menu. Now select "transaction reports."

From the transaction report menu, select the "trial balance" option. You will then see a listing of the accounts that have just been entered into the general ledger. The debit and credit balances for these charts will be zero, since no account balances or other entries have been made in these accounts.

JOURNAL ENTRIES

All entries to a general ledger accounting system are made through the journal. This includes opening balances for both balance sheet and profit and loss accounts. On a periodic basis the journal entries are reviewed by the accounting department, and then these entries are posted to the general ledger. Until such time as they are posted, the general ledger does not reflect these new entries.

We will now move through this procedure step by step.

To begin, select the "transaction" option from the main menu. From the transaction menu, select "journal entry." Several examples of journal entries are given later in this case. Do not enter them in your computer. They are given as examples only. Later in the case (in the "Assignment" sections) you will have the opportunity to make actual entries.

To determine whether an entry in the journal is recorded as a debit or credit, use the following guidelines:

> o Sales are recorded as a credit.
> o Expenses are recorded as debits against the
>   appropriate expense account.
> o An increase in an asset is recorded as a debit.
>   For example, if $100 cash is received, a debit
>   of $100 is made against the cash account.
> o An increase in a liability account is recorded
>   as a credit. For example, an increase in the
>   accounts payable account is recorded as a
>   credit.
> o In double-entry accounting, the debits equal
>   the credits.

Example One

Thomas purchases $10,500 of spring seedlings.

Step 1. Debit purchases 10500.

Purchases

_____

10500 |

Step 2. Credit the liability account, accounts payable, for 10500.

Accounts Payable

| | 10500

Example Two

Thomas sells $2325 of products to a wholesale account.

Step 1. Debit accounts receivable.

Accounts Receivable

2325 |

Step 2. Credit sales.

Sales

| 2325

Example Three

Thomas receives a check in payment for the last wholesale order.

Step 1. Credit accounts receivable for 2325.

Accounts Receivable

| 2325

Step 2. Debit cash for 2325.

Cash

2325 |

JOURNAL LISTING

After a series of journal entries has been made, it is customary to obtain a hard copy (printed) of the journal before these entries are posted to the general ledger. In this system, to obtain a listing on either the screen or printer, return to the report menu and select "transaction reports." From the next menu, select "journal listing."

This journal listing is considered the audit trail for journal entries, and in most systems this must be printed before the process of posting can proceed. An **audit trail** is a listing of the entries made in the system, so that the entry can be traced from its first step to its last.

If any errors are uncovered in the journal listing, the only way corrections are allowed in this and commercial systems is to return to the journal entry stage and make new entries in the journal (these are often called adjusting entries) to offset the error. For example, if you intended to credit accounts receivable for $200 but entered this as a credit to accounts payable, then the adjusting entry would include a debit to accounts payable of $200, and a credit to accounts receivable of $200. In another example, if you debited the cash account for $1000 when the entry should have been only $100, the adjusting entry will be a credit for $900.

GENERAL POSTING

After it has been determined that the entries in the journal listing are correct, then you are ready for the next step in the accounting cycle, called posting. In the posting process the entries in the journal are added to the existing balances of the general ledger accounts.

From the main menu select the transaction option, and from the next menu which appears select the journal posting option. Once this choice is made the posting process is automatic. It requires no user input.

After posting has been completed, the journal entries have been incorporated in the general ledger accounts and the journal no longer has any entries. This prepares the journal for a new round of journal entries.

TRIAL BALANCE

After posting has been completed, a trial balance can be obtained by returning to the transaction report menu. This trial balance should be examined carefully. If errors are found or if the total debits do not equal credits, then the source of the problem must be located and adjusting entries made through journal entries. Then these adjusting entries must be posted to the general ledger. The purpose of this tedious process is to ensure that audit trails are maintained whenever changes are made to the general ledger. Otherwise changes could be made with no way of tracing when they were made and who made them.

ADDING AND DELETING ACCOUNTS

Adding new accounts or deleting current accounts can be undertaken from the maintenance menu. New accounts can be added to an existing chart of accounts at any time. However, an account cannot be deleted unless its net credit balance is zero. If it is not zero, then adjusting entries must be made through the journal before the account can be deleted.

ASSIGNMENT ONE

The purpose of this assignment is to initialize the accounting system and customize the accounts to correspond with the user's system.

1. Build the chart of accounts with the accounts currently in use and listed in the case.
2. Using journal entries, enter only the balance sheet figures as of December 31, (see Figure 2 in Part One of the Thomas case).
3. Obtain a journal listing.
4. Correct any errors by making adjusting journal entries.
5. Obtain a new journal listing.
6. Post these entries to the general ledger.
7. Obtain a trial balance. Do debits equal credits? If not, make adjustments through the journal.
8. Obtain a balance sheet.

At the conclusion of this session, the accounting system is ready to be used in the next accounting period.

ASSIGNMENT TWO

The purpose of this assignment is to enter several transactions for the current acccounting period.

1. A sale is made on credit for $2500.
2. Sales are made for $1000 cash.
3. A customer pays part of their bill by sending Thomas a check for $500.
4. Wages are paid out of the cash account for $752.
5. Thomas purchases $2500 of seedlings from a grower in Florida. The bill is due in 30 days.
6. General expenses, including advertising and promotion, are incurred for $300.
7. A sale is made on credit for $2000.
8. A customer pays their bill by including a check for $2500.
9. After making these journal entries, obtain a journal listing. Correct any errors through adjusting journal entries.
10. Make another journal entry. A sale is made on credit for $1200. Obtain a new journal listing. Has the entry just made been included?
11. Post the journal to the general ledger.
12. Obtain a trial balance and compare it to the trial balance obtained in Assignment One. Can you verify the differences?
13. Obtain a journal listing and explain the result.

THOMAS GREENHOUSES INC. (PART THREE)

In this final part of the Thomas Greenhouses case you will have a chance to learn how an end-of-period closing is accomplished by using the software which accompanies this case.

END-OF-PERIOD CLOSING

At the end of an accounting period (monthly, quarterly or yearly), several entries are made to the chart of accounts that constitute the closing process.

One step in this process involves the determination of the cost of goods sold for the most recent period. We will do this for Thomas by making adjusting entries to the Purchases, Inventory, and Cost of Goods Sold accounts.

Returning to the balance sheet totals and transactions covered in the previous parts of the case, these accounts now have the following balances.

PURCHASES	INVENTORY	COST OF GOODS SOLD
2500 I	2000 I	I

Step 1. Close purchases to the Cost of Goods Sold account. This is done by crediting purchases for $250 and debiting cost of goods sold for the same amount. The purchases account now has a zero net balance.

PURCHASES	INVENTORY	COST OF GOODS SOLD
2500 I 2500	2000 I	2500 I

Step 2. Close opening inventory (Inventory account) to the Cost of Goods Sold account.

PURCHASES	INVENTORY	COST OF GOODS SOLD
2500 | 2500	2000 | 2000	2500 |
		2000

Step 3. Enter ending inventory (usually obtained by a physical count) by debiting Inventory and crediting Cost of Goods Sold. Let us assume that a physical count reveals an ending inventory of $1,500.

PURCHASES	INVENTORY	COST OF GOODS SOLD
2500 | 2500	2000 | 2000	2500 | 1500
	1500	2000

Notice that the Purchases account has a zero balance and that the Inventory account now reflects the beginning inventory level for the next accounting period. What is the balance of the Cost of Goods Sold account? What does this balance represent? It represents the cost of goods sold in this recent period.

The next step in the end-of-period closing process is to make adjusting entries for depreciation of capital equipment. Let us assume that depreciation for this period was computed separately to be $1500. The journal entry would then be to debit _____ for 1500 and credit _____ for 1500. In filling in these blanks, use only the chart of accounts already established earlier in the case.

COMPLETING END-OF-PERIOD CLOSING

After the end-of-period adjusting entries have been made, a trial balance is obtained to ensure that no errors have been made. Are the entries correct? Does the debit balance equal the credit balance? If the answer is yes, then the End-of-Period Closing program can be initiated. This is accessed from the transaction menu. And like the posting process, operation is automatic.

The purpose of the End-of-Period Closing program is to determine net profit for the period and credit this amount to the retained earnings account. This procedure will also set the profit and loss accounts to zero and thereby reset the system for the next accounting period. It's all automatic once the posting option is selected from the menu.

After the End-of-Period Closing program has been run, obtain a new trial balance and verify that the changes in the profit and loss accounts and in the retained earnings accounts have been made.

FINANCIAL STATEMENTS

Financial statements for the previous period can be obtained at any time after a period has been closed. From the main menu select the "report" option. From the report menu, select financial reports. Finally, from the financial report menu select either a profit and loss statement or a balance sheet.

NEW YEAR

After the end-of-period closing has been completed, entries for the new period can begin at any time.

ASSIGNMENT THREE

The purpose of this assignment is to guide the user through a sequence of end-of-period entries.

1. Obtain a trial balance. Do debits equal credits? If not, uncover the source of the problem and make adjusting entries to the journal, followed by another posting process.
2. Depreciate $1000 of plant and equipment.
3. Close purchases and beginning inventory to the cost of goods sold account.
4. Ending inventory has been estimated to be $1700. Make the appropriate adjusting entries.
5. Obtain a journal listing. Are there any errors in it? If so, correct them through journal entries.
6. Post these entries to the general ledger.
7. Obtain a trial balance. Make any necessary corrections.
8. Run the End-of-Period Closing program.
9. Obtain financial statements.
10. Compare the new financial statements to the ones presented at the beginning of the case. Verify the differences.

11. Obtain a trial balance. Notice that the retained earnings account has been updated to reflect the profits for the period and that the balances in the profit and loss accounts have been set to zero. The system is now ready for the next period.
12. To illustrate that the system is ready for the new period enter a cash sale for $500 in the journal. Obtain a journal listing, post the entries to the general ledger, and obtain a trial balance. It should be clear that this sale for $500 is the only sale in the general ledger. In other words, this new period's entries have begun and the profit and loss accounts have started from a zero balance.

MANAGEMENT INFORMATION SYSTEMS

A **Management Information System** (MIS) provides the kind of information that business professionals need to manage an organization and make decisions. This section presents three cases concerning Management Information Systems. In the first, Yarmouth Inc. explores the need for timely information to increase the productivity of its sales staff. Bristol Furniture, a made-to-order manufacturer, is the subject of the second case. Bristol Furniture has one type of Management Information System in place and a need for a shop-floor-control system. In the third case, Sanborn Company, a medical electronic equipment firm, has a solid transaction system foundation for a Management Information System, and makes plans for using a wealth of untapped internal and external data to better support management decisions.

YARMOUTH INC.

The division manager, Lisa Harwood, had just told Dan Tobin, director of marketing, that the productivity of the sales staff had to increase. The statistics Harwood referred to came from a recent trade magazine. They suggested that the sales staff at Yarmouth was performing well below industry averages. Average order size per salesperson, for example, and the number of calls per day were about half those reported by other companies in the same business.

"Dan, we've got to act now or we'll never hit our profit goals for the quarter," Harwood said. "Can you get back to me tomorrow with some ideas on how we can show some fast improvement?"

Tobin had been with Yarmouth Inc. for six years. He was hired as a salesperson and last spring was promoted to director of marketing.

Yarmouth produces a line of industrial cleaning equipment including vacuum cleaners, waxers, and polishers, and maintains a staff of 142 salespeople who call on industrial accounts within a several hundred mile radius of their homes.

Tobin went home that evening concerned about his ability to make the changes that were needed. On the ride home it occurred to him that he could give the staff a pep talk but it probably would have only a short-term effect. Without close supervision, they were on their own, and any effort to manage their performance from this distance was difficult. The only hard data he had were the monthly sales reports, which he received nearly a month after the reporting period closed. The January sales data, for example would be received at the end of February. Perhaps, he thought, he might get these data sooner. Then he could respond faster to those who weren't getting the job done.

CONSULTING THE MIS DEPARTMENT

Tobin's first stop the next morning was the MIS department. There he told Maurice Brown, director of MIS, about his problem.

"We're not your problem," Brown said. "You are. The data coming in from the field travel at a snail's pace. Your salespeople fill out order forms and then a few days later put them in the mail. Before the sales data show up here and are entered by data entry clerks into the sales order entry system, the data are sometimes several weeks old. Then, after the goods are shipped it takes another few weeks for the data to be entered by data entry clerks into the sales history database. The report we send you accesses the sales history file, and until that file is updated, we can't send you your monthly reports. If the past is an indication of the future, I'm afraid the best we can do is get you a report within a month of the end of the period, unless, of course, you get your orders in here quicker."

Although Tobin was not confident that Brown could help him obtain more timely data, he went on to explain some additional information he needed to maintain closer control over the sales staff.

NEW APPLICATIONS

"Maurice, last night I sketched a few reports that would help me maintain tighter control over the sales force. These reports would let me scrutinize their efforts much more closely. And I think the information the salespeople would get from these reports would help them to schedule their time more effectively and do a better job."

Tobin showed him two reports -- sales diary, and sales productivity analysis.

SALES DIARY

The sales diary would report the number of calls per day for each salesperson, the number of hours per day that the salesperson spent with prospects, the number of sales calls year-to-date, and the cost per call.

SALES PRODUCTIVITY ANALYSIS

The order analysis report would include, for every salesperson, the cost per call, revenue per call, revenue to expense ratio, and the call to close ratio. The call to close ratio is the number of total calls made divided by the number of calls that resulted in a sale.

Tobin finished describing these reports. "Maurice," Tobin asked, "how long do you think it would take for you to begin producing these reports on a weekly basis?"

"Dan, I don't understand your logic. If I use the current sales history database to produce your reports, I might be able to get them to you a few weeks after the data are in that database, but you have just complained that a report like this would be too out-of-date to be useful."

QUESTIONS

1. Describe the problem expressed by Harwood.
2. Would you consider the current sales order entry system a transaction system or a Management Information System?
3. Describe the difference between a transaction system and a Management Information System.
4. How would you classify the system Tobin is exploring -- transaction system or MIS?
5. Is the sales information that Tobin currently receives timely? Is timely information in this situation necessary?
6. Do you think there is anything that Brown can do while still using existing software and hardware, that will improve the timeliness of the data Tobin receives?
7. Do you agree with Brown that this is Tobin's problem?
8. Describe the reports Tobin wants.
9. Often the kind of data desired from an MIS have not been previously collected as input data and stored in the database. Does the case suggest that this may also be the situation with Tobin's new system? Give an example of any data you think would have to be collected and entered into the system before these reports could be produced.
10. Management Information Systems produce both full reports, which include selected data from all the records in a file, and exception reports, which include only data on those situations that are out of control. Suggest an exception report that might be appropriate in the system Tobin is considering.
11. Management Information Systems are used by many levels in the managment hierarchy, from the lowest level, called operational planning and control, to the top level, called strategic planning. In operational planning and control the focus is on the planning and control of daily activities. In strategic planning the focus is on long-range issues. Would most of the applications Tobin is considering be classified as operational planning and control or strategic planning?
12. How do you think Harwood would respond to the suggestion of a completely new MIS for marketing?

13. Describe a completely new system -- one that uses source data automation and on-line processing -- that might meet Tobin's needs more effectively than the present one.
14. Can you briefly describe the benefits and costs that might be associated with a new system? Do you think benefits might exceed the costs? Why?
15. How would you proceed with this problem?

BRISTOL FURNITURE

Bristol Furniture is a manufacturer of living room and bedroom furniture. The company's products are sold in over 2000 stores and are considered by many to represent the best quality available in the marketplace.

When customers purchase Bristol Furniture from a retail showroom, they can select from an array of over 350 different furniture designs in as many as 130 different fabrics. Since it would be costly to keep all designs in all fabrics in stock, Bristol manufactures to the customer's order.

To keep track of customer orders, process these orders, maintain control over production facilities, and process routine accounting transactions, Bristol has developed an integrated computer information system. Development of this system began over six years ago, in response to increasing paperwork costs and a lack of control over operations. First, accounting applications were introduced; then sales order entry, inventory control, and production planning and control applications were added.

The benefits from these applications have played a significant role in management's ability to manage the company well and maintain healthy profit margins while growing at a rate of 10 percent per year. Shortly after these computer applications became operational, inventory levels dropped 10 percent and lead times shortened by 50 percent. The result: lower production costs and faster customer deliveries.

ACCOUNTING SYSTEM

The accounting system at Bristol -- the first function which they computerized -- is an **on-line transaction processing system** which includes general ledger, accounts receivable, and accounts payable software. The general ledger system has over 300 accounts, designed in such a way as to support cost center accounting. The accounting data from this system can be used to prepare reports that show how actual costs in different cost centers compare with the budget for these areas and also how the costs compare with those incurred in previous years. The system also supports routine acounting transactions and produces profit and loss statements and balance sheets.

When the manufacturing cost centers were established, the decision was made to identify each major step in the production process as a cost center. Steps include kiln drying, rough cut, finish cut, assembly, upholstery, quality control, storage, and shipping. Cost centers were also established for accounting, marketing, design, and personnel.

INVENTORY

The inventory system maintains data on the stock levels of some 5000 items -- called **stockkeeping units** or **SKU**'s -- used in the manufacture of the furniture. Such items include the different types (oak, pine, spruce, and so on) and lengths of wood; mechanical parts such as swivels, nuts, and bolts; and upholstery fabric.

Terminals are located in the stockroom and shipping area. Whenever a part or finished product is added to or removed from stock, a clerk makes an entry into the system. Users in other areas, such as in purchasing or production scheduling, can also inquire about the status of a part or finished item from terminals in their area. They can find out how many items are in stock, how many are on order, and when the items ordered are due.

Periodic inventory reports are also available from central data processing. One report prints the items that are out of stock, another lists inventory investment for each category of SKU, while another even summarizes those items for which there has been little or no demand.

MANUFACTURING PLANNING

Bristol can be classified as a made-to-order manufacturer. This means that manufactured items are produced to fill specific orders. When sales are made, the order is received by order entry clerks and is entered into the computerized sales order entry system. From the order entry database the order data are used in the production scheduling process. This made-to-order manufacturing method is different from the made-to-stock method used by clothing and household appliance manufacturers, where units are produced for the purpose of restocking inventory, not for a specfic customer who is waiting for delivery.

Every month the scheduling department at Bristol prepares a master production schedule (MPS) on the computer. Similar products -- such as recliners, in which the only difference is the fabric and the electric heat and massage unit -- are "batched" so that there will be some efficiencies when these pieces of furniture are produced. The schedule specifies the finished product category to be manufactured and the planned shipping date.

In the next step, the production department uses the computer to translate the orders for finished products into a detailed production schedule. This schedule specifies when parts must be ordered from suppliers, when parts must be produced in Bristol's own production faciilities, and when assembly, upholstery, packing, and shipping must take place. And the computer software is written in such a way that the dates on the schedule assure that these steps begin at the right time and in the correct sequence so that the finished product will be completed according to the date on the master production schedule.

What complicates the development of this detailed schedule is that each of the finished products is comprised of many parts and several subassemblies, where a subassembly -- like the frame of a table -- is an assembly of parts. A bill-of-materials file organizes this detail. The file, which is stored on disk, not only identifies the parts and subassemblies for a given product, but it shows the order in which they are assembled, and also includes an estimate of the time it takes to complete each step in the process.

When the detailed scheduling process begins, the bill-of-materials file is accessed. Using this file as a reference, a software package, called a material requirements planning system (MRP), works backward from the planned completion date on the master production schedule to determine when each item, subassembly, or finished assembly must be started so that the due date for the product will be met. The outcome of the MRP system then becomes the detailed production schedule.

SALES ORDER ENTRY

Bristol has an automated sales order entry system. When an order arrives, the order data are entered into one of the terminals in the sales department. After the appropriate computerized credit checks, the order is stored in the order file and awaits scheduling. If at a later time the customer calls and asks for a status report, the order entry system can access the master production schedule to determine when the order is scheduled to be shipped.

MANAGMENT INFORMATION SYSTEM

The staff at Bristol keeps in touch with performance through several regularly scheduled reports including monthly sales performance charts, profit and loss statements, and the inventory reports described earlier. Some of these are called exception reports, which only include those activities or results which are beyond the limit of expected results. One exception report, the cost overrun report, lists profit centers whose costs exceed budgeted levels. But management can also request data by accessing the database using an English-like **query language**. With this language they can obtain information to solve an unusual problem or to monitor a potentially troublesome area for which regular reports are not available.

SHOP FLOOR CONTROL

One category of information, however, is not available. Once a job is released to manufacturing and the production of several units begins, it becomes very difficult to follow the progress of the job including all the parts, subassemblies, and final assembly. After the job has been started, the next time it shows up on the computer system is when the finished unit is sent to the warehouse area for packaging and shipping. What this means is that if the schedule falls behind or bottlenecks occur -- as they frequently do -- then management will usually first learn about it well after it has happened.

A shop floor control system would require terminals throughout the manufacturing facility. Whenever jobs were released to production and whenever they moved from one manufactuing cost center to another, it would be necessary for data about the job, such as the number of pieces in the lot and the task completed, to be entered into the terminal. The data would be sent from the terminal into the central computer and update the shop floor control database. Users could enter the job code for any job on the floor and then learn its whereabouts as well as other information such as the number of steps remaining or the number of pieces in the batch.

Management has made it clear that the investment in this new system will lead to better control over the flow of jobs through the facility. In addition, marketing will be able to query the system so they can respond when customers want to know how long it will be before their furniture is shipped.

QUESTIONS

1. Describe the business that Bristol is in.
2. What impact did the development of a computer information system have on Bristol's performance when it was first installed?
4. Describe the accounting system.
5. **Management Information Systems** are those that support routine problem solving and decision making. Usually an MIS produces regular reports. Which applications at Bristol can be categorized as MIS? Explain how the transaction system is a backbone for the accounting MIS.
6. Describe the inventory system. How many items are covered by the system? What are these items called? How are transactions entered?
7. Can the inventory system be classified as a transaction system, an MIS, or does it support both uses? Explain.

8. Is Bristol a made-to-order or made-to-stock manufacturer? Explain the difference.
9. What is the first step in the production scheduling process? Is a computer used?
10. Explain the master production scheduling process.
11. What is the bill-of-materials file? How is it used by Bristol to produce a detailed schedule?
12. Explain the purpose of an MRP. What input data are needed? What output does the MRP produce?
13. Explain the sales order entry process. Would it be classified as a transaction system or MIS?
14. Explain the difference between the scheduling system and the proposed shop-floor-control system.
15. What benefits would be derived from a shop-floor-control system by the production department? By the marketing department?

SANBORN COMPANY

Sanborn Company manufactures and distributes medical electronic equipment used in hospitals, labs, and physicians' offices to diagnose and monitor health-related problems. The product line includes blood analyzers, electrocardiograph machines, heart monitors, and defibrillators.

Products are sold through two distinctly different channels. Sanborn maintains its own staff of 14 salespeople assigned to five different regional sales offices. In addition, their products are carried by 137 distributors.

INFORMATION SYSTEMS IN PLACE

Sanborn Company is no stranger to sohpisticated information systems. Accounting and manaufacturing systems at Sanborn have been in operation for over a decade. The manufacturing system supports a range of manufacturing functions from purchasing to production scheduling and inventory control. The accounting system handles general ledger accounting, billing, accounts receivable, accounts payable, and payroll.

In addition to accounting and manufacturing information systems, Sanborn also maintains a sales order entry system. Orders obtained by the sales staff are directly entered into their own portable computers and sent to headquarters through the telephone network.

When Glenn Stiskal was recently promoted to marketing manager, it was clear that the reason he was chosen for the job was because he is a strong advocate of marketing information systems. Before he came to Sanborn, two years ago, he worked for IBM in a division which made extensive use of such systems.

A WEALTH OF UNTAPPED DATA

During his two years with Sanborn, Stiskal often expressed his approval of the sales order entry system, but equally often voiced his concern over management's lack of initiative in the development of more sophisticated applications. He pointed out that the sales order entry system included a wealth of information that should be used to monitor, control, and plan sales activities. But marketing actually did little with the data, even though it was possible for them to access the database using a query langue. Using this language, however, would require training and few were willing to take the time to learn.

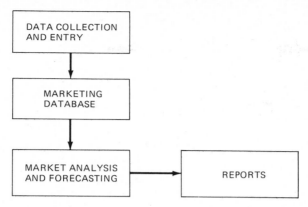

Figure 1. The proposed system encompases the collection, storage, processing, and presentation of data

Today, the first day of the semi-annual national sales meeting, Stiskal met with the three regional managers, whose responsibilities included managing the 14 people on the sales staff as well as working with the 137 distributors who carried Sanborn products. He would use this opportunity to launch his new project. "Within the next few weeks I plan to submit a project proposal to management that will help us do a better job of managing the sales function. The system I propose will include four modules," Stiskal said. "The first is a marketing database, the second is a system that tracks and updates the data in the database, the third is a market analysis and forecasting module, and the fourth a collection of reporting programs." The system is shown in Figure 1.

MARKETING DATABASE

"The marketing database will include internal and external data. **Internal data** will come from several sources. They will come from our present sales order entry system, and they will also come from manufacturing and inventory databases which we already maintain in the production division. But we will also include data about our current customers, prospective customers, and even about our competitors. The **external data**, that data which is collected and maintained by commercial database services, will include market data, economic data, demographic data and general industry data."

DATA TRACKING AND ENTRY

"The second module will focus on the collection and entry of data into the database. Its responsibility will be to keep the internal data up-to-date.

"The tough part will be to assign individuals to these tasks and to institute new procedures for collecting data from the field. We will have to set up systems for collecting and entering data about customers, and our competitors. For example, someone will have to monitor the characteristics of the equipment and prices our competitors are charging for equipment that is similar in function to ours and then enter these data into our system. One possiblity is to require the sales staff to undertake periodic surveys in their market area, while another is to hire a person for whom this will be their major responsibility."

MARKET ANALYSIS AND FORECASTING

"The next module in our system," Stiskal continued, "will support market analysis and forecasting. Here is where we process the data in the database. For example, at each of our semi-annual meetings I expect to be able to show you a five-year demand forecast for each of our products. Every month we will compare and display graphically the difference between our market share in several product areas and the market share achieved by our major competitors. The Market Analysis and Forecasting Module will include the software necessary to do this analysis."

REPORTS

"The fourth module will produce the reports we need to manage our business," Stiskal said. "To us, this is the most important part of the system. What we need more than anything else are good reports that are produced on a regular basis. As you all know, the system we're using now doesn't work because we don't have the time to enter requests using a query language we don't understand. With regular reports we will get our information automatically."

At this point Cheryl Miller, the eastern regional manager, interrupted. "Glenn, why are we going to all this trouble to collect more data? We've got plenty in the sales order entry database."

"Yes, we do have lot of data, but its not always the data we need. Let me give you an example. To do a better job at these meetings, we need to watch industry trends better than we are doing now. The most cost-effective way to do this would be to subscribe to services that provide us with access to trade association data and government statistics on health care. With these data we will be able to monitor these trends and learn more about the changing medical needs of the population, and about general economic conditions that will influence the demand for our products. Right now we fly by the seat of our pants and act only after our competition acts. I want us to act first not react later.

"And I might add, Cheryl, that data isn't the only issue. I've already emphasized the fact that we desperately need useful and timely reports. My proposal will help us reach that objective."

"Can you give us a few examples of the kinds of reports you have in mind?" asked Larry Ebert, the western regional manager.

"Two kinds of reports, routine and exception. Both will be produced on a regular basis -- weekly or monthly. The routine reports will include a complete summary of a marketing activity. For example, a weekly sales report will be produced that lists all products, and then compares the quantity sold with the sales targets for that sales period. And we will produce a report that lists the sales staff and summarizes their sales by product line for the recent period. Other reports will include market share data, customer plans for buying new equipment, competitive pricing comparisons, and market trends, to name a few. The exception reports will include only those events that are out of line with expectations. For example, we will have an exception report for products with sales more than 20 percent below targeted levels. Or we might produce exception reports for those customers who have not received a sales call in more than six months, or a list of customers to whom credit can no longer be extended because their accounts are overdue."

Janice Theodore, the southern regional manager, thought that the project was too ambitious. "We're already overworked. It seems to me that since we haven't taken the time to learn the query language and as a result don't use the sales database, we probably don't need access to that data. Don't you think it's possible that your project will create a lot of paper but have little impact on sales? I've heard about several expensive computer applications that are seldom used. This could be one of them."

Ebert showed his concern. "Glenn I disagree with Janice and feel your on the right track, but don't you think we ought to be more involved with these plans. After all, we are the ones who will use the system.

QUESTIONS

1. As the current sales order entry system exists, would it be classified as a transaction system or Management   Information System?
2. How are transaction systems and Management Information   Systems related?
3. How does a database support an MIS?
4. Describe the marketing database in the new system. What data will it include? What is the difference between internal and external data?
5. What external data will the system access? How will it be collected? How will it be used?
6. Differentiate between the types of data and information that data entry clerks would need to do their job and the kind of data that would be used by marketing professionals to plan and control sales and marketing activities.
7. What types of reports would the MIS produce? Give several examples

8. Miller has suggested that the external data that will be collected by the system may be unecessary. Do you agree?
9. Theodore suspects that this system may not be very useful. Explain her position. Do you agree?
10. Ebert feels that the staff should be more involved if such a system is developed. Do you think the development should be in the hands of Stiskal who has considerable experience in this area.
11. Do you think that an MIS in which routine reports are produced can meet all the needs of the business professionals in the marketing department, or should they also learn how to use the query language so that they might obtain data not available in report form? Support your answer.

GRAPHICS

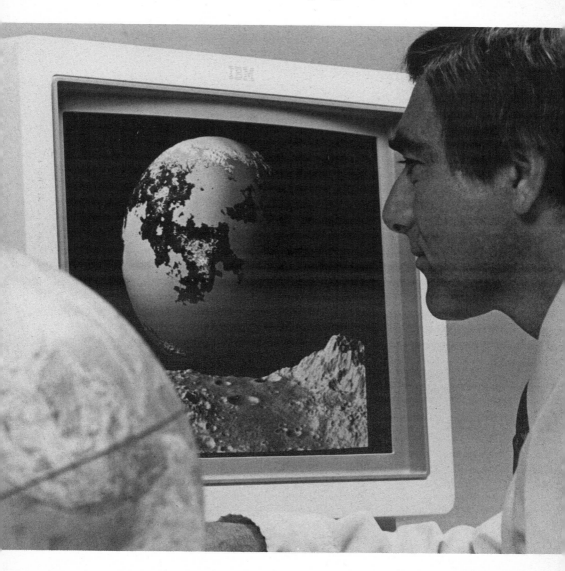

"A picture is worth a thousand words" is true for much computer output as well. Reports can run not only to a thousand words but to a thousand or more pages, which frustrates anyone trying to dig relevant information out of them.

Computer graphics refers to the presentation of computer stored data in graphical form. Early computer systems had few graphics capabilities, and even more recent systems have offered only poor facilities. But with the coming of end-user computing, database management systems, spreadsheets, sophisticated graphics software, and high-resolution output devices, the use of graphics has mushroomed. The data to be used in graphics are now more readily available; contemporary software makes it easier for business professionals to describe the graphics desired; and current hardware produces a high-quality product.

At Franklin Power and Light, the case presented in this section, a praiseworthy Management Information System is in place. Output from the system is in the form of voluminous reports that are often, to put it charitably, ignored. Franklin faces the need to embody its MIS output in concise graphics that will help the goals of the system to be realized.

FRANKLIN POWER AND LIGHT

Franklin Power and Light Company, serving several midwestern states, is known as one of America's best-managed utilities. One reason for this reputation is Franklin's extensive use of a computer system to support managment decisions.

Eleven years ago they began producing a biweekly chartbook that summarized, graphically, the key data that management needed to plan and control operations, but at that time they were prepared manually and relied on data that were often out-of-date. Sometimes the charts were too out-of-date to be useful.

About seven years ago Franklin began producing regular computer reports and at that time discontinued the costly process of drawing the charts. The data in these reports were in many cases the same data used to prepare the old charts, but because the reports could access timely data from the database, they were more up-to-date. The major problem, however, was that these reports contained so much data that they were seldom read. And busy executives found it impossible to quickly scan the reports to learn of troublespots that needed closer scrutiny.

The reports cover four different areas of management responsibility. They include Energy Customer Forecast, Material Management Inventory Tracking, Nuclear and Fossil Fuel Production, and Customer Service.

ENERGY CUSTOMER FORECAST REPORTS

The Energy Customer Forecast Reports are used in the process of forecasting demand over the next several month period. One report includes actual daily demand figures for residential and commercial power for the most recent month. Another report includes the daily demand trend for the last twelve-month period, a third report summarizes the monthly demand over the last ten-year period, and a fourth report includes data on demographic trends in the region and the effect of energy conservation programs.

MATERIAL MANAGEMENT INVENTORY TRACKING REPORTS

The purpose of the Material Management Inventory Tracking report is to encourage careful control of inventory while providing better service levels to Franklin customers. The report, produced monthly, lists each part in inventory, its balance, and the demand for that part over the last month. Another column shows the year-to-date demand for the part.

NUCLEAR AND FOSSIL FUEL PRODUCTION REPORTS

The utility has two nuclear and eleven fossil fuel plants. The Nuclear and Fossil Fuel Production reports summarize statistics from these operations. The power output statistics include the daily power output from each plant for the previous month. Also included is a column that shows output for the same period last year, and another column for year-to-date figures. Another report summarizes several safety statistics which, if they fall within a certain level, would suggest that the plant is operating safely. These safety levels are based on the recommendations of the Institute for Nuclear Power Operations. Another report summarizes the operating budget for each facility and compares these figures with budgeted targets. Still another report computes the cost per customer of supplying power and compares these figures with costs one year ago.

CUSTOMER SERVICE REPORTS

The Customer Service reports include the data needed to monitor customer service levels. One report includes the average time it takes for a repairperson to respond to a customer call for service. Another summarizes the length of time it takes for a customer to have a question answered on the telephone, including all waiting time if a customer service rep is not available. And a third report summarizes the length of time it takes for a new customer hookup.

BACK TO CHARTS?

Although the charts Franklin used seven years ago were easy to read, they were often out of date, and always expensive to prepare. The reports used today, while less expensive, are more difficult for manangement to use. Most managers use them infrequently if at all. Many make their way to the large, circular output file near the desk.

When Gregg Hall, a senior systems analyst, returned from this year's COMDEX convention in Atlanta, he wrote a memo to his boss, Tanya Moy, describing a new graphics system he had seen. The system made it possible to access mainframe data and produce a wide variety of bar, line, and pie charts.

Hall explained that it would make more sense to use the data in the database to produce charts than to produce reports with hundreds and hundreds of numbers.

The graphics software he saw could access these data and do the job professionally and quickly.

This software had many features that eliminated the painstaking details needed to access central data and create graphs from these data in the past. Not only did the software relieve the designer from the data access details, but it also made it easy to establish the right scale for each graph, to put several graphs on the same page, to superimpose one graph on another, to select one of 20 different print styles called fonts, and to adjust the text printed on the chart so that if the chart were made larger or smaller the text could easily be read.

CHARTBOOK

Hall also described a presentation by a restaurant chain in which they explained a chartbook that they had developed. It was a spiral-bound notebook of operating results expressed in graphical form, prepared monthly and distributed to managers at each of their locations.

"If we can use this new graphics software and put together a chartbook that displays our management data in an attractive and easy-to-use format, we're bound to improve our decision making performance, customer service, and the bottom line," Hall said.

QUESTIONS

1. How would you classify the applications of graphics in this case, as a transaction system or MIS? Why?
2. How were the old charts prepared? What was the problem?
3. Do the current reports include up-to-date or out-of-date data?
4. Do you think the system that Hall has seen at the convention should be considered for use by Franklin?
5. Summarize the advantages of the system that Hall has described.
6. Do you think it is important that a graphics system have the capability to access mainframe data? Why?
7. What is a chartbook?
8. By referring to the applications described in the case, list all of the charts that should be included in the chartbook.
9. Describe the data in the Energy Customer Forecast reports. For what applications and in what way would you expect management to use these data? Would line, bar, or pie charts be appropriate?

10. Describe the data presented in the Material Management Inventory Tracking Reports. For what applications and in what way would you expect management to use these data? Could line, bar, or pie charts be used?
11. Describe the data presented in the production report. For what applications and in what way would you expect management to use these data? Could line, bar, or pie charts be used?
12. Describe the data presented in the Customer Service Reports. How would you expect these data to be used by management? Would you choose a line, bar, or pie chart if you were to show these data graphically?
13. The sophistication of graphical output varies from very simple, such as a black-and-white line chart, to very elegant, such as a three-dimensional color chart. Do you think the sophistication of the output is important in this application? In which applications is it most important?
14. Write a short paragraph justifying your recommendation.

ARTIFICIAL INTELLIGENCE

It is true that computers cannot match the intelligence and common sense of a human being. But it is also true that computers are being used today to help human beings make better decisions, not only in computer research laboratories but in a variety of organizational settings.

Artificial intelligence (AI) refers to the use of computers to simulate some of the characteristics of human thought such as reasoning, inference, learning, and problem solving. One of the fastest-growing areas in information technology, artificial intelligence finds its way into the corporate world primarily in the form of expert systems. An **expert system** is a computer information system that uses knowledge obtained from experts and makes the experts' point of view available to nonexperts.

In the case in this section, Hillside Bank was recently merged into Century State Bank. In comparing notes, officers found less consistency at Hillside than at Century where approval or denial of loan applications was concerned. The possibility is explored of using an expert system to help establish a common approach throughout the bank.

CENTURY STATE BANK

Shortly after the merger of the the Hillside Bank into the Century State Bank, the operations department at Century began reviewing the methods and procedures followed by both banks in the process of providing services to their customers. Where duplicated efforts were found, the intent was to centralize functions wherever possible, and if this where not possible then the intent was to at least make sure that the the methods and procedures followed throughout the expanded organization were consistent.

LOAN PROCESSING

One of the first areas to be reviewed was loan approval and processing. The staff at Century found that the application and approval process at Hillside was much less formal than their own. There seemed to be less consistency with the approval or denial of loan applications at Hillside than at Century.

THREE CHOICES

There were three points of view to solving this problem. The first was to continue with the loan processing operations at Hillside locations but bring Hillside loan officers into Century for training. The second possibility was to consolodate all loan processing at Century and terminate this service at Hillside locations until some later date. The third option was to develop an expert sytem that would help establish a consistent approach to loan applications throughout the organization.

EXPERT SYSTEMS

As Pat Hardee, one of the MIS professionals from Century's staff, explained at meeting of senior loan officers, "**Expert systems** are a category of computer applications that make an expert's point of view available to a nonexpert. They are designed by compiling some of the knowledge of the experts in a particular field, like senior loan officers, and then providing this knowledge to people who might not be quite as knowledgeable, junior loan officers as an example."

"We generally consider building an expert system when certain conditions apply," Hardee continued. For example, if a difficult problem has already been solved by experts and will need to be solved regularly by nonexperts; if the expertise needed to solve a problem is not distributed evenly in the organization; if a consistent approach is needed to solve similar problems; or if complex problems in ambiguous environments must be solved, then we consider an expert system."

"Our loan granting process seems like a perfect application for these systems," she added. "And I would suggest that we build the system around a shell."

EXPERT SYSTEM SHELL

An expert system shell is a developmental tool for building an expert system. It can be visualized as a prefabricated general framework into which specific knowledge about an application can be placed. The user must do some of the work to develop the system for a specific application, but many of the details are left to the shell software.

"If we don't use a shell," Hardee explained, "then we would have to build a custom expert system from scratch using a language such as LISP or PROLOG, a process much too time-consuming and expensive for our application.

"The type of shell I have in mind is called an induction shell. In this approach the expert's knowledge, called the knowledge base, must be capable of being expressed in a decision-matrix format. A decision-matrix is similar to the layout of a spreadsheet, in that it has columns and rows. First the factors that the expert or group of experts considers when making a decision are entered into the matrix. Then several "training examples" are entered, the purpose of which is to "suggest" how the experts used these factors to reach a decision. Next, the system's built-in " inference engine" -- specially designed expert system software -- uses the training examples to determine or "induce" the rules the expert probably followed when making the decision for those training examples.

"Once trained and once the shell has "learned" a set of rules, it is ready for use. Then loan officers from different bank locations will be able to enter specific data obtained from a loan applicant and discover whether or not an expert would have accepted or rejected the application."

When Hardee was asked to explain the system in more detail, she went to the chalkboard and drew a table that she called a decision-matrix. She asked the group for examples of the kind of data they considered when screening an applicant. She was told that they collected data on age, number of years of education, how much the customer owed on their car, monthly car payments, whether they rented or owned, how much their monthly rent or mortgage payments were, combined monthly income, credit card debt, and net worth.

AGE	# OF YRS EDUCATION	CAR LOAN BALANCE	MONTHLY CAR PAYMENTS	RENT OR OWN	MONTHLY RENT OR MORTGAGE	COMBINED MONTHLY INCOME	CREDIT CARD DEBT	NET WORTH		ACCEPT OR REJECT
20	11	1250	100	R	325	1065	0	1400		R
36	16	——	——	O	975	4260	1675	41000		A
51	10	——	——	O	360	1840	3160	1000		R
31	18	2165	250	R	750	3600	2250	3450		A
42	16	750	175	R	650	2050	3675	2500		R
48	16	1100	210	O	750	3900	1400	85000		A

Figure 1. When an expert system shell is used the data are collected and entered using the format of the table shown above.

She explained that when they finally designed the system they would sit down and review the factors they used when reaching a decision more carefully, but for now they would use these as an example of the way the system is put together.

Across the top of the table she listed the factors that had just been suggested. Then she went around the audience and asked each of the senior loan officers to give her the data, to the best of their recollection, for a recent applicant. The data she filled is shown in Figure 1.

Hardee then explained that to develop the expert system, she would enter the factors like the ones they had described, and then enter the data for each example including the decision reached by the loan officer. When completed, the inference engine would then be instructed to induce the rules that were most consistent with the data. Then the system would be ready for testing.

To test the system it would be necessary for the 'experts' to enter several test examples to see if indeed the recommendations made by the system were consistent with the outcome they would expect. If the recommendations were not consistent with expectations, then it would be possible to return to the design stage and enter more training examples.

QUESTIONS

1. What is an expert system?
2. Describe the induction method. How is an expert system shell used?
3. What is an inference engine?
4. Describe the steps in building an expert system that uses the induction shell method.
5. Explain the purpose of training examples?
6. How would an expert system help the loan-granting process at Century?
7. Should Century build a custom expert system?
8. Expert systems can handle ambiguous situations in which no clear-cut decision is suggested or in which decisions that have been made for training examples appear to be in conflict. Does this mean that expert sytems have no place in important decision processes like the approval or denial of loans?
9. Should nonexperts who use these systems rely on them completely? Explain.
10. Suppose the expert system, after it has been developed, does not seem to produce the kinds of decisions with which the experts feel comfortable. What do you think would be the problem, and how could it be rectified?
11. Describe the three points of view for solving the problem at Century. Which would you recommend? Why?

COMPUTERS AND SOCIETY

Beyond doubt, computers have brought benefits to diverse areas of our lives. They have probably had more positive than negative impact on our workplace, jobs, standard of living, safety, education, and health.

One area of concern to many people is **privacy**. We can define privacy as the assurance to individuals that the information gathered about them is accurate, will only be used as intended, and will somehow be protected from improper and unauthorized access and use.

The case in this section concerns the FBI's National Crime Information Center (NCIC). Decades old, this center stores an impressive amount of information about many people. Plans to expand the system with access to new databases and more efficient query techniques have drawn praise from law-enforcement officials but alarmed some members of Congress, the American Civil Liberties Union, and private citizens.

N C I C

The 30-member advisory policy board had recommended a plan for modernizing the 20-year-old information system at the FBI's National Crime Information Center (NCIC). While there were those who felt that an overhaul of the system was long overdue, there were others who felt differently.

CURRENT SYSTEM

The NCIC was created by the FBI in 1967. At the heart of this system is a computer that maintains over 15 million records, or one record for about every 15 Americans. The files include information on missing persons, arrest warrants, stolen property, criminal histories, registered guns, and registered vehicles.

Access to this database is widespread. Using remote terminals the database can be accessed from 17,000 terminals located throughout the country. These terminals provide the means by which 64,000 federal, state, and local police agencies, government prosecutors, and judges can access the system.

PLAN

At the present time the FBI is considering a proposal submitted by their advisory policy board in which a dramatic expansion of the system is recommended. This proposal recommends that the scope of the system be enlarged to include on-line links to outside databases and the creation of new databases, as well the capability to provide access to the system's users in new ways.

The board's preliminary plan would create a new database to help law enforcement authorities track the movements of criminal suspects across state lines, as well as track the movements of individuals on parole or probation, convicted terrorists, foreign spies, vehicles "of investigative interest," and people who are the subjects of any criminal investigation.

The expanded system would also be capable of establishing on-line access to numerous federal databases including social security records, immigration and passport records, the FBI's fingerprint files, and files on financial securities, registered weapons, and federal prison inmates.

The proposal also recommends that data be stored on the "known group membership" of wanted individuals, that information on misdemeanors and juvenile crimes be added to its criminal history files, and that an improved method be developed of searching the database to increase the number of "hits" from a query -- such as by permitting inexact matches and allowing searches by nickname and by modus operandi. In addition, the expanded system should have the ability to transmit photographs, fingerprints, signatures, and other images.

But the board was sensitive to the issue of privacy. It rejected a proposal to track "associates" of criminal suspects, and also rejected a proposal to obtain on-line access to private databases such as credit bureaus, airline passenger lists, and telephone records.

SUPPORT

The plan has strong support from law enforcement officials, many of whom believe that the system should be updated to take advantage of the latest in computer technology, especially the ability to link computers so that a wide spectrum of data can be made available when needed. These backers feel that updating the system and providing better information to the nation's law enforcers will be a decisive move in response to the public's demand for stronger measures against criminal activity.

OPPOSITION

But a spokesperson for the American Civil Liberties Union (ACLU), a group whose goal it is to safeguard the rights of individuals, sees it differently. He feels that this proposal would allow authorities to create "electronic dossiers on citizens" and that these dossiers could easily be abused.

According to an interview with this spokesperson, the FBI used the NCIC in this way to track antiwar and civil rights demonstrators in the early 1970s, until this activity was later disclosed to the public and condemned by members of Congress.

The ACLU spokesperson has urged Congress to enact legislation restricting the NCIC to information already on the public record, such as arrest warrants, stolen property reports, and criminal history records.

While some members of Congress approve the plan, others are more sensitive to the concerns raised by the ACLU. One legislator from California, a frequent opponent of expanding the NCIC, has planned to hold hearings on the issue when the House of Representatives reconvenes in the fall.

CONCERNED CITIZENS

Individuals too have spoken out against the plan. One legislator received a letter from a constituent expressing concern for a national database that would likely contain incorrect data. She referred to a study conducted by the U.S. Office of Technology Assessment, in which NCIC arrest records were sampled and their accuracy checked. The study found that 27 percent of the records in the sample did not include information about the outcome of the case. And she added that other studies of state criminal data have shown that up to 75 percent of the records are incomplete or incorrect.

"How can we be sure," she concluded her letter "that data accuracy will improve? Incorrect data of this nature can be very damaging to the individual. From the evidence we have seen I think that if you consider both the innocent and guilty who will be affected by this system, we will be better off without the new system."

In another letter an individual uncovered the fact that in 1973 the U.S. Department of Health Education and Welfare (now the Department of Health and Human Services) issued a report that warned of the dangers of databases that might invade a person's privacy. In that report the department stated that

> We recommend against the adoption of a nationwide, standard, personal
> identification format, with or without the SSN, that would enhance the
> likelihood of arbitrary or uncontrolled linkage of records about people,
> particularly between government-supporte automated person data systems.

The writer went on to argue that the government had already warned about the dangers of linking records and the dangers to privacy this would impose, yet here the NCIC is proposing to do just that.

Another letter from a police commissioner of a large city explained how the use of the current NCIC system had significantly helped in the solution of many crimes. He said, "If we're serious about cracking down on crime, this new system is a must."

QUESTIONS

1. What is the NCIC?
2. Describe the purpose of the proposed system.
3. What new data would the new system store?

4. What external data sources would be accessed by the new system?
5. Give some of the arguments in favor of the proposed system.
6. Who seems to be in favor of the new system? Who has voiced opposition?
7. Do you think that incorrect and innacurate data present a problem in the new system? Assume that you are in favor of the new system; how would you respond to this criticism?
8. Do you think the system will threaten an individual's right to privacy?
9. According to some, the NCIC system was misused when it tracked antiwar protesters and civil rights activists in the early 1970s. Should this alleged misuse of the system, which happened long ago, influence the consideration of the new system today? Why or why not?
10. Suppose that you figured out a way to make long distance calls without being charged for them. After running up over a thousand dollars in charges you were caught, charged with a misdemeanor, and fined. With an expanded NCIC system you would have a criminal record that could be accessed from any location in the country. Do you feel this would unjustly interfere with your rights to keep some information about your past quiet? What would be your reaction if prospective employers could gain access to this database?
11. "Even if 25 percent of our records are inaccurate, the system will still help to track dangerous criminals." How would you respond to this statement?
12. Write a paragraph (or more) expressing your position on the expanded NCIC system.

G L O S S A R Y

Access time
The time is takes to retrieve or store data on a disk, measured in milliseconds.

Accounting system
A computer system that collects, stores, processes, and presents an organization's accounting data.

Accounts payable system
A computer system that maintains records of purchases made from vendors.

Accounts receivable system
A computer system that keeps track of the amounts owed by, and the payments received from, customers who make purchases on credit.

Application software
A collection of programs that direct the computer to perform user-related tasks such as payroll, inventory control, or accounting.

Arithmetic/logic unit (ALU)
The function within the CPU responsible for performing arithmetic and logical operations on the data as specified by a program.

Artificial intelligence
The use of the computer in certain limited application areas to simulate some of the characteristics of human thought such as reasoning, inference, learning, and problem solving.

Audit trail
A record of the details surrounding the use of an application, which can be used to trace the use of an application and can also be used to reconstruct where and how a particular problem occurred.

Balance sheet statement
A report produced by a computer accounting system that lists the assets and liabilities of the organization. The data for the report are obtained from the general ledger accounts.

Bar code
A data input technology in which identification data -- in the form of lines of varying thicknesses -- are affixed to an item and read with an optical wand.

Batch processing
Processing an identifiable job, such as payroll, as one work unit.

Binary
Pertaining to a number system that uses 1s and 0s.

Broadband system
A system using coaxial cable that can carry hundreds of data paths. Used in local area networks.

Byte
Group of adjacent binary digits (usually eight) that are operated on by a computer as a unit.

Cell
The intersection of a row and column in a spreadsheet.

Central processing unit (CPU)
The computer itself. It accepts data, stores the data in temporary storage, processes the data, and sends them to an output device.

Centralized data processing
The organization of the data processing function in such a way that most of the activities are located and managed in a centralized environment.

Character
A letter of the alphabet, a number, or a symbol.

Chart of accounts
The accounts in a general ledger system.

Coaxial cable
A transmission medium like the cable that brings cable TV into homes. It has a central core surrounded by a shield and can transmit large volumes of data.

COBOL
Common Business Oriented Language. A computer language developed for business applications that require a significant amount of file processing.

Communication system
The hardware and software that links computers with terminals, printers, and other computers.

Computer
An electronic device that operates under the instructions of a program, and can accept data, process them, and present the results as output.

Computer information system
A particular kind of computer system used to collect, store, process, and present information to support an organization.

Computer system
The computer itself together with support equipment, programs, procedures that users follow, and people who use the system.

Controller
A specialized computer used to supervise and coordinate data traffic in a communication system.

Conventional file processing
Use of traditional computer languages like COBOL and BASIC rather than the use of a database management system to process files.

CPU
See Central processing unit.

Data
Raw facts that are entered into the computer.

Database
A nonredundant collection of data stored in one or more files.

Database management system (DBMS)
A set of programs that manages and controls a database, providing the mechanisms through which data items can be stored, retrieved, and changed.

Data dictionary
A separate file in a database management system that stores such data as the name of each data item, data structure for each item, programs that use each item, and level of security for each item. Used to facilitate the development and use of a database.

Data integrity
The state of accuracy or legitimacy of data in a database.

Data processing
A systematic sequence of operations performed on data to accomplish an objective.

DBMS
See Database management system.

Desktop publishing
The use of specialized hardware and software to produce hard copy of a quality similar to that obtained by commercial printing.

Direct access systems
Computer systems in which data are stored on disk and can be accessed almost instantly.

Direct file processing
Processing data using a direct access system. An approach to data processing in which the data are processed instantly.

Disk
See Magnetic disk.

Distributed processing
A computer system in which computers and storage devices -- in different physical locations -- are linked together for the purpose of sharing programs and data.

Dot-matrix printer
A printer with a movable print head that encases a set of wires. When each wire is activated, the end of the wire presses against the ribbon and prints a small dot. Combinations of dots are used to represent characters.

Downloading
The process of sending data and even programs from a central computer to a remote computer.

Dynamic data
Data such as bank balances which change frequently.

Electronic filing
Creating, storing, and retrieving the documents in an office environment.

Electronic data processing (EDP)
Using computers to process data automatically.

Electronic mail
A system in which documents are instantly transmitted from one terminal or microcomputer to another terminal or microcomputer in electronic form.

End-user
Person who is using the computer information system for transaction or decision making purposes.

End-user computing
Solving problems using a computer oneself without involving programmers or other professionals.

Expert system
A computer information system that uses knowledge obtained from experts and makes the experts' point of view available to nonexperts.

Expert system shell
A prefabricated general framework into which specific data surrounding an application can be entered, after which the shell itself develops an appropriate expert system.

Fiber optic cable
A cable used for communication that is made up from thousands of clear glass fibers about the thickness of a human hair. Transmission speeds approach the speed of light. Used in local area networks as well as long distance communication.

Field
A collection of one or more related characters, where a character can be a letter, number, or symbol.

File
A collection of related records.

File manager
A category of data management software that is easy to use but permits only one file to be open at a time.

Floppy disk
A flexible magnetic disk enclosed in a protective envelope and used mainly with microcomputers.

Fourth generation language
A language that requires the user to specify what is needed rather than the details of how it is to be done.

General ledger
The collection of accounts for maintaining records of an organization's accounting transactions.

Graphics
The use of symbolic input or output from a computer including lines, curves, and other geometric shapes and forms. Requires terminals, plotters, printers, digital scanners, and other interface devices.

Hard copy
Computer output that can be considered permanent, usually referring to paper or document output.

Hard disk
A magnetic disk built on a rigid base which has a higher storage capacity and faster access than a floppy disk.

Hardware
The computer system's physical equipment.

Hybrid topology
A description of the physical layout of a network that combines both ring and star topologies.

Indexing
The use of a reference file in direct processing to find the location of a record stored on disk. The index stores the record's key and its physical location on disk. When records are accessed by users, the index is first searched to find its location.

Induction shell

Type of expert system in which the factors used by the experts to make a decision are entered into the system. Next, several "training" examples are entered. Then the system automatically induces the rules that the experts probably used when making the decisions in these training examples.

Input

Term relating to a device or process involved in the entry of data into the computer information system, or to the data themselves.

Information

Data that have been processed into a form that is useful for decision making or problem solving.

Information system

See Computer information system.

Ink-jet printer

A nonimpact printer that uses nozzles which spray liquid ink on a page.

Internal data

The data collected by an organization in the process of doing its business. These data may be maintained centrally or locally.

Inventory system

A (computer) system which keeps a record of the number of items stocked by an organization.

KB (kilobyte)

1024 bytes.

Key

A field used to identify a record.

Knowledge base

Experience of experts stored by an expert system as data and rules.

LAN

See Local area network.

Laser printer

A nonimpact printer that operates much like an office copy machine. Capable of high-quality black-and-white reproduction at high speeds.

Laser wand

Input device that reads bar codes by scanning them with a beam of light.

Local area network

A collection of computers, usually microcomputers, connected together within a limited geographic area, such as a building, for the purpose of sharing data and programs.

Logical view

The way in which users visualize data and data relationships, in contrast with the way data are physically stored in the computer and on secondary storage devices.

Magnetic disk

A flat circular platter on which data can be stored using a magnetic process and from which data can be retrieved.

Magnetic tape

A flexible flat plastic ribbon on which data and programs can be permanently stored, and from which they can be retrieved.

Main memory
That part of the CPU in which temporary storage of programs and data occurs while an application is processed.

Mainframe
The largest computer used by most organizations. Mainframes have the largest main memories, the fastest processing times, support massive secondary storage, provide access to many users, and are usually centralized.

Management Information System (MIS)
An information system that provides the kind of information that business professionals predictably need to manage an organization and make decisions.

MB (megabyte)
One thousand kilobytes, or 1,048,576 bytes.

Menu
A screen, or part of a screen, listing the program options that can be chosen.

Microcomputer
A small, self-contained computer with one or more disk drives for secondary storage.

Microsecond
One-millionth of a second.

Millisecond
One-thousandth of a second.

Minicomputer
A computer whose capacity and capabilities are between a mainframe and a micro.

MIS
See Management Information System.

Module
A design element in the structure chart that includes a collection of steps necessary to perform an information-processing task. A discrete and identifiable unit of hardware or software that is used with other units in the system.

Mouse
An interface device, moved in the palm of one's hand over a desk surface, and used to move or "point" the cursor to a menu selection. Also used to draw shapes or illustrations on a flat surface such as a desk. These shapes simultaneously appear on the terminal screen and can be stored for later use.

Multitasking
The ability of a computer system to perform many tasks at what appears to be the same time. Each task may require the use of a different program or several users may share the same program but be involved in different activities.

Multiuser software
Software used in a network that permits several users access to the programs and data in the system.

Network
An interconnected group of computers, terminals, communications equipment, and communications facilities used to support data processing activities.

Off-line data entry
The process of data entry in which data are grouped and entered as a batch into the computer system.

Off-the-shelf system
Application software that has been developed by a software vendor for a specific commercial application and must be used exactly as written.

On-line data entry
Immediate processing, by a CPU, or data entered into a computer system.

On-line processing
An approach to processing data in which the data entered into the system or requested by the user are processed instantaneously.

On-line transaction processing (OLTP)
An approach to processing transaction data in which the data entered into the system or requested by the user are processed instantaneously.

Operating system
Part of the system software that coordinates the functions performed by the comptuer hardware including the CPU, input/output units, and secondary storage devices.

Optical disk
Circular disk that stores data as microscopic patterns that can be read optically. Storage capacity is high but access time is slower than magnetic disk.

Password
A set of characters, such as a number or word, assigned to an individual, which permits that person access to a computer or to a limited subset of applications on the computer.

Payroll system
System used to process a payroll.

Physical view
The way data are actually stored in the computer and on secondary storage devices, in contrast to the way they may be viewed by users.

Pixel
One of the dots of light on a display screen that make up the image displayed.

Point-of-sale terminal
Data entry terminal located at the point of sale.

Primary storage
See Main memory.

Profit and loss statement
A report that summarizes the profit or loss associated with a specific accounting period. Data for the report come from the general ledger.

Program
A sequence of instructions written in a computer language that tell the computer what to do.

Prototyping
The use of special-purpose application development software to develop a small-scale version of an application so that it can be tested early in its development cycle.

Query language
A language, usually fourth generation, used by end-users to access a database for informal requests.

Record
A collection of related fields.

Record format
A general description of a file that includes the identification of each field in the record, the length of each field, the type of data, and the identification of the primary key.

Redundancy
The storage of the same data item in more than one physical location in a database.

Relational DBMS
A database management system in which the data are entered as tables and are related when the database is used or when reports are produced.

Relational operator
An algebraic sign such as <, >, or =. Used in a database management system when specifying the criterion by which records will be selected when a file is searched for data.

Relationship
A term used in database processing to express the linkage between a record in one file and one or more records in another file.

Resolution
The clarity of output on a screen measured by the number of picture elements -- called pixels.

Ring topology
A network configuration in which each computer is directly connected only to its neighbor on either side. The standard topology of local area networks.

Risk
The range of possible outcomes to which a decision maker is exposed if a certain alternative is chosen.

Schema
An overall representation or description of every data item to be included in the collection of files found within a database.

Secondary storage
Storage on tape or disk. Storage not maintained in the CPU.

Sensitivity analysis
Exploring the consequence of "what if" questions on the outcome of an alternative.

Sequential access
Data accessed in a specified sequence according to the order in which they have been stored on secondary storage media.

Sequential file organization
Records stored in some predetermined sequence, one after the other.

Sequential file processing
Processing data using sequential access methods.

Software
The collection of programs used to provide instructions for the operation of a computer.

Source data automation
The process of automating the data entry process in such a way that data are collected as close as possible to their source.

Spreadsheet
A software package that accepts data in the form of columns and rows and facilitates their manipulation and presentation.

Star topology

The physical layout of a network in which every computer or device is linked to a central computer which controls the sharing of resources in the network.

Static data

Data such as a name and address that change infrequently.

Stockkeeping unit (SKU)

An item stored in inventory.

Structured design

The use of certain guidelines, tools, and techniques to ensure a disciplined and cost-effective approach to the development of an application.

Structured programming

An approach to programming that uses certain guidelines and tools to ensure a cost-effective and successful completion of the job.

Structured/unstructured view

A view or classification of an information system in which the application is classified by the characteristics of the decision problem itself. When using a structured system a well-defined sequence of steps is followed by the end-user. This is not true of unstructured systems.

Supercomputer

The largest and fastest type of computer, used in government, defense, and sometimes by large organizations.

System control

Safeguard built into an application during the development process to ensure data accuracy, data security, and protection from unauthorized users.

Systems development process

The steps or cycle followed to develop a computer information system, consisting of systems analysis, systems design, program development, and system implementation.

System software

A collection of programs that manages the resources of the entire computer system and provides supporting functions for the application programs.

Systems analysis

A preliminary study of a proposed system to determine if the project has any merit, followed by a detailed analysis of the system's requirements.

Systems design

The detailed steps necessary to convert the requirements of new systems into a collection of working programs, and to test and implement the new application.

Tape

See Magnetic tape.

Template

A worksheet in which all of the labels and formulas, but none of the data, have been entered for a particular application. It then becomes a reusable shell.

Third generation language

A procedural computer language such as BASIC or COBOL.

Topology

Pertaining to the physical layout of a network.

Track
The physical location where data are stored on tape and disk.
Transaction processing system
A computer system used to process the routine day-to-day information flows in an organization.
Twisted wire pair
A pair of copper wires like the wires used to connect telephones in the home or office.
Voice input
The process of directly entering computer data or instructions using the human voice. The system must be trained to recognize an individual's pronunciation of a specified and usually limited vocabulary.
Winchester technology
Pertaining to a hard disk permanently enclosed to protect it from environmental contamination.
WORM (Write-Once Read Many times) optical storage system
An optical disk on which data or programs can be written just once by the user, but which can be read any number of times.